100 Days of Scrum

By Beverly Reynolds

Book Summary

100 Days of Scrum is designed to breakdown the Scrum framework into 100 daily pieces of information. That is, you can read one page per day or breeze through the pages at your own pace. Either way, you will gain a clear understanding of the Principles, Aspects, Processes and Phases of Scrum and all of the events, key terms and order of precedence.

You will also see acronyms (identified by *ACR* in italics at the beginning of a line or section), charts and visual images in numbered figures, keyword definitions, job aids and even practice test questions by the end of this book.

If something is important, I have tried to emphasize the text, bold it or put it in all capital letters.

There are plenty of places provided amongst the text for you to write your notes as well.

I hope that after reading this book, if you like the materials, please share it with your friends and provide feedback.

BONUS!

As a thank you for purchasing this book, you also get a discount code for the Using Scrum: Implementation Strategies course on Udemy.com: BOOKSALE17 (**WHILE SUPPLIES LAST**).

DAY 1:

Scrumstudy Exams

These Scrum details are designed to give you an overview of the key terms and to help you pass your exams. Providing you with the tools to aid you in your success is our job; however, passing each exam is your responsibility. That is, running through this book or any of our other resources one time simply is not enough.

We recommend that you study and make notes in the spaces provided. There are several images throughout this book to aid you in your studies.

ACR This book provides a firm foundation of Scrum as the basis for the following exams (as of this writing):

- *SFC – Scrum Fundamentals Certification*
- *SDC – Scrum Developer Certification*
- *SMC – Scrum Master Certification*
- *SAMC – Scrum Agile Master Certification*
- *SPOC – Scrum Product Owner Certification*
- *SSMC – Scaled Scrum Master Certification*
- *SSPOC – Scaled Scrum Product Owner Certification*
- *ESMC – Expert Scrum Master Certification*

Proctored Exam Requirements

ACR Scrumstudy allows each of the exams to be proctored exams. That is, before you schedule your exam online or through an *ATP (Approved Training Partner),* you must have an online webcam device.

For information on the exams, see Scrumstudy.com.

TIP: Typically exams are scheduled in the UTC time zone.

DAY 2:

The SBOK Guide
ACR *SBOK stands for Scrum Body of Knowledge.*

The SBOK Guide is a document that outlines and provides guidance for implementation success of continually-changing projects, programs and portfolios. We will tell the difference between a project, program and portfolio very soon as well as provide an example for each.

It is several hundred pages in length and provides even more details than this book can provide.

FREE Download

The SBOK guide can be downloaded online and serves as a set of rules – regardless of industry, size of organization and type of project or product being created. You can get a free download of this SBOK Guide using the link below:

http://www.Scrumstudy.com/SBOKGuide/download-free-buy-SBOK

Good luck on your exams!

DAY 3:

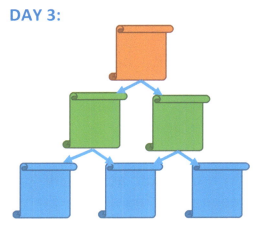

Figure 1: *A diagram of the relationship between Portfolios (at the top), followed by Programs, and then, Projects at the bottom.*

Projects, Programs and Portfolios

A project is a collaborative effort to produce a feature, product or service based on a vision statement and value to the Customer.

A program is a grouping of related projects. Each project could have one or several sub-projects.

A portfolio is a grouping of programs that are also related and are in place to deliver specific business benefits across an organization.

Now let's discuss an example of each:

- You work for a fashion clothing company that would like to allow Customers to login and have the system remember the sizes and styles that they purchased in the past. This is an example of a technology development PROJECT.
- If this same company is to implement a multi-faceted site for selling clothing for the first time, they are doing much more than implementing a new feature. This would be an example of a PROGRAM, or group of several projects by several teams.
- Finally, if that same company wants to make wide-spread changes across all of their sub-companies and every single website, this would be considered PORTFOLIO management.

Scrum Overview

Scrum is a FRAMEWORK (this is an important word!) for creating and maintaining a consistent rate of work (which can be measured in Velocity) for complex projects, programs and portfolios based on the ever-changing needs of the Stakeholders or business.

Scrum Teams are typically small in size. If a Scrum Team has more than three to nine members, it is typically broken into additional Scrum Teams. Smaller teams can knowledge-share more easily than larger teams.

Scrum is still the most popular of the Agile methodologies. That is, it is <u>NOT</u> the only Agile method of development.

Since you know how a project is defined, let's move onto the structure. A project typically has multiple sprints. Each sprint outputs an increment of work that may or may not have a release of code. The idea behind a Scrum sprint is that a potentially shippable product is produced by the end of each sprint.

There are many benefits of implementing Scrum as your project management framework. Scrum Teams tend to be collocated or work out of the same location. If across multiple locations, then conference calls become essential.

Scrum also allows you to respond to changes more rapidly by having work assigned to a single sprint based on what are called User Stories, which illustrate who will use the feature being developed and the scope of the feature – at a high level.

Another essential benefit of this framework is the idea of collaboration. Scrum fosters positive contribution by helping to work as a team in terms of collaboration and accountability.

In tomorrow's detail, we will discuss the sprints of a project.

DAY 5:

The Sprints of a Project

Let's take a more specific look at the term sprint. This is a key concept and building block within the Scrum framework.

A sprint is a time-boxed block of time that a project is divided into. That is, there are time limits set for each sprint within the timeframe of the entire project. Scrum activities that are time-boxed, such as sprints, tend to have less overhead and tend to have a more efficient development process day-to-day.

Each sprint starts with the Sprint Planning Meeting and includes time to develop the features and products for the current sprint. In Scrum, less planning for the project is done at the beginning of the project.

Keep in mind, Scrum is also heavy on team work and has less of an emphasis on detailed documentation. That is not to say that documentation is not created, it is just not the focus.

Now that you know the structure of a Scrum project, let's breakdown the lifecycle of a Scrum project, highlighting several of the key terms in order starting with the Project Business Case and ending with the Accepted Deliverables.

Notes:

_____

_____

_____

_____

_____

_____

DAY 6:

Project Business Case	Project Vision Statement	Prioritized Product Backlog	Release Planning Schedule
Justification Why does the user need this feature, product or service?	Goals that should be measured	Contains increments of work User Stories and Epics	2H/W High-level only

Figure 2: A table showing an overview of the lifecycle of Scrum (continued in *Figure 3*). The details are read left to right.

Sprint Backlog	Daily Standup Meetings	Create Deliverables	Accept Deliverables
A list of items or features in a sprint	Scrum Team mandatory What did I complete yesterday? What will I complete today? Impediments?	War Room Preview to Stakeholders	Acceptance determined by Product Owner

Figure 3: A continuation of the table showing an overview of the lifecycle of Scrum. The details are read left to right.

Scrum Lifecycle Overview

On the previous page, there are two tables that provide a high-level overview of the main milestones of the project lifecycle.

Each project must begin with justifying the existence of the project. There are several milestones along the way leading to the acceptance and successful implementation of deliverables to the end user.

The end user is anyone that will be benefitting from the system, project or outcome of the product. On the next day, we will detail the lifecycle of a Scrum project.

It does <u>NOT</u> contain all key terms you need to know, nor does it provide each detail about the terms discussed. It is simply meant to give a high-level overview. You will read these terms over and over throughout this book.

Prior to a project kickoff, a Project Business Case must exist. A business case is created to determine the feasibility or existence of the project. At this point, there is no development of work, as even the team members have not yet been selected.

This topic is continued on DAY 7.

Notes:

_____

_____

_____

_____

_____

_____

DAY 7:

Scrum Lifecycle

Continuing from yesterday's topic, the Project Vision Statement will be crafted explaining the goals of the project. At this point, the team is starting to take shape as the vision is being formed.

Once the team is successfully in-house, a list of high-level features called the Prioritized Product Backlog is devised. The items, otherwise known as User Stories and Epics, are brainstormed and listed for the entire life of the project. As the project progresses, items or stories are broken down and prioritized into sprints. Each sprint has a pre-determined block of time, which means it is time-boxed, to one to six weeks each, based on the complexity and scope of the project.

A Release Schedule is put in place with major date milestones for when code will be released. Not every sprint will have a release of code.

The Prioritized Product Backlog is ultimately prioritized, with the highest priority items or features being worked first and added to the first sprint. These items are further tracked in the Sprint Backlog.

Therefore, you will notice there is a Prioritized Product Backlog as a collection of items for all sprints combined AND a Sprint Backlog, for items to be attained and developed in the current sprint. As we stated before, nowhere in this book do we mention that all of the planning is done at the beginning of the project with LOTS of documentation.

At the dawn of each sprint, the team will look at the potential items and finalize or even reprioritize; however, items are never added to the Sprint Backlog during the current sprint, but items CAN and ARE added to the Prioritized Product Backlog.

TIP: Be sure to read the previous paragraph one more time.

This topic is continued on DAY 8.

DAY 8:

Scrum Lifecycle (continued)

In each sprint, the team meets daily in a Daily Standup Meeting regarding the progression of sprint items. This meeting is limited to 15 minutes and it is held at the same place at the same time to maintain a consistent and sustainable pace.

The rest of the day is spent together, in close proximity, sometimes two people to the same computer for knowledge sharing and sometimes in a dedicated place, such as a War Room. This is how deliverables are approached and created.

At the end of each sprint, the product deliverables are inspected by key Stakeholders based on a demo. Feedback is given and the team looks at what was successful and what was not successful.

Now that you have a base knowledge of Scrum at a 50,000 foot level (give or take), let's talk about the core roles of Scrum in tomorrow's detail.

Notes:

_____

_____

_____

_____

_____

_____

DAY 9:

Figure 4: *A representation of the Scrum core roles.*

Scrum Core Roles

In Scrum, there are core roles and non-core roles. Let's focus on the core roles first.

TIP: This is an important concept, regardless of the exam.

Product Owner Characteristics

We will begin with the Product Owner – since they typically kickoff the project. This individual is responsible for the following:

1. **ACR** *Achieving maximum business value, ROI (Return on Investment) and OBJECTIVES for any project, no matter the type, industry or organization*

2. *Communicating with senior management during the project*

3. *Ensuring the Scrum Team understands the features that are most valuable to the Customer and what it will take for each*

4. *Deemed as the negotiator and able to make decisions and react based on the project goals*

5. *Understanding at a high level, the flow of Scrum as it relates to the Customer AS THE VOICE OF THE CUSTOMER*

TIP: Remember specifically what I just said, the Product Owner is the VOICE OF THE CUSTOMER.

DAY 10:

Scrum Master Characteristics

While the Scrum Master is a management role, this person is more known as a facilitator. Scrum framework promotes teamwork and team ownership by the clearing of roadblocks or impediments.

Notice that there is no position of Project Manager. A Scrum Master is to display a <u>SERVANT LEADER</u> approach. They are to:

1. *Listen as challenges or impediments are brought forth*

2. *Have empathy to the concerns of others*

3. *Possess the ability to heal after disagreements*

4. *Ability to persuade and to bring others' to a conclusion*

5. *Conceptualization when analyzing problems*

6. *Foresight to learn from the past*

7. *Stewardship without controlling*

8. *Commitment to assisting others in their own growth*

9. *Building a sense of community - to be a <u>SERVANT</u> first*

Monumental progress so far!

Notes:

_____

_____

_____

_____

_____

_____

DAY 11:

Scrum Team Characteristics: Paired Programming

A Scrum Team typically consists of three to nine people. The members may take part in what is called <u>PAIRED</u> <u>PROGRAMMING</u>, by where two people may sit at the same computer and develop a user story feature or item together for collaboration and learning.

That being said, each team member must not only be great in a specific area of development, but also knowledgeable in other areas too – or be willing to learn from other team members. The team as a whole is responsible for the final implementation of all deliverables.

Now let's take a look at the non-core roles of a Scrum project.

You are well on your way through the contents of this book!

Notes:

_____

_____

_____

_____

_____

_____

DAY 12:

Figure 5: *A representation of the Scrum non-core roles.*

Scrum Non-Core Roles

The roles detailed here are called non-core because they do not actually do the day-to-day project work. They may simply interact with the Scrum Team members. These roles are definitely interested in the lifecycle of the project, but are not responsible parties with a formal role. However, these roles SHOULD be taken into account in the planning of the project and/or individual sprints.

ACR   The Scrum Guidance Body is typically known as the SGB.

The SGB is an optional role and could be a set of documents or experts that define objectives regarding quality, government regulations and security. The day-to-day work is done by core roles.

You already know what a Product Owner is, but a Chief Product Owner is a role presiding over multiple Scrum Teams in larger projects. This individual facilitates the work of multiple Product Owners. You also already know that Product Owners themselves are a key role, but the Chief Product Owner is a non-core role. The Chief Product Owner tracks the business viability of the larger project – throughout the life of the project.

This topic is continued on DAY 13.

Scrum Non-Core Roles (continued)

A Chief Scrum Master facilitates Scrum activities, just like a single Scrum Team Scrum Master, but again, on a larger scale. This role takes a lot of coordination amongst teams.

Stakeholders is sort of a generic term for Users, Customers and Sponsors. These individuals typically influence the final outcome and result of a project – not just at the end of a project, but all throughout the project lifecycle.

Vendors are the organizations or sometimes even individuals that provide or offer products or services that do <u>NOT</u> fall within the competencies covered by the project.

Now let's look at how the Scrum Team manages conflicts that arise in a project.

Congratulations on making it to this point!

Notes:

_____

_____

_____

_____

_____

_____

DAY 14:

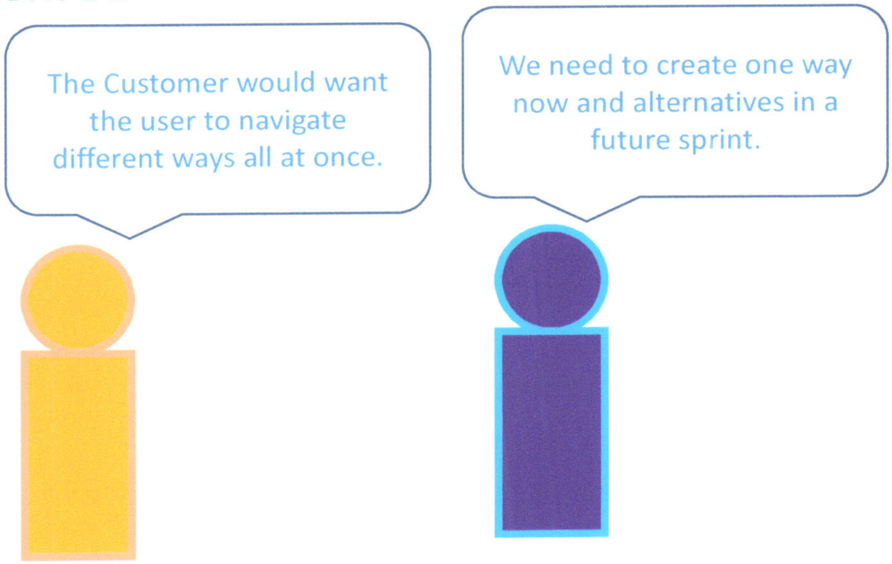

Figure 6: A representation of conflict management within the lifecycle of a project.

Conflict Resolution

There are several approaches for conflict resolution. It is often such that the hardest part of a project is dealing with personalities.

There are four approaches to conflict resolution. Let's look at the first option of <u>WIN-WIN</u>. In this approach, conflicts are approached with open communication. Both people are willing to talk out the issue to come to agreement. This means that not only do both individuals need to be willing to work it out, but the organization must create an environment conducive to this happening as well.

The next approach is <u>LOSE-WIN</u>. This is when one party in the disagreement does not feel as if they are being heard or their opinion matters. This happens when the other person is taking an authoritative approach to the discussion. One person wins and the other loses. The Scrum Master should encourage those who feel they do not matter and may have withdrawn.

This topic is continued on DAY 15.

Conflict Resolution (continued)

The next is <u>LOSE-LOSE</u>. This is where both persons are parties in an argument settle for less than optimal results without fully coming to the best solution for the project. In this approach, both people lose. Scrum meetings such as the Daily Standup Meeting, Sprint Planning and other meetings are put in place with structure to avoid this from happening – such that agreements and conflicts can be brought forward to the team for the best possible outcome and solving, for the betterment of the project as a whole.

The final approach is <u>WIN-LOSE</u>. This is when one Scrum Team member believes his or her viewpoint is perhaps more important than the other person's view. One person may have a sense of competition in mind. Keep in mind that even the Scrum Master is more of a facilitator than a manager. Everyone on the Scrum project is to be thought of and treated as an equal contributor. If someone needs to learn about a specific tool, functionality or means for organizing code, it is the collective responsibility of the team to ensure knowledge is shared and each member feels as though they are working in a safe environment.

Next, we will visit the Scrum principles.

Notes:

_____

_____

_____

_____

_____

_____

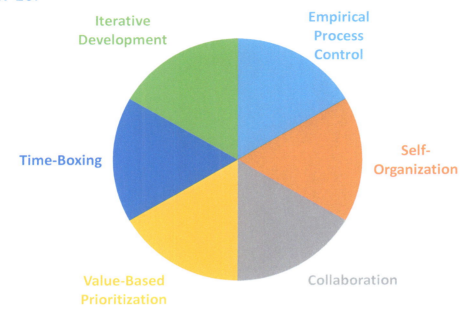

Figure 7: *A chart depicting the six Scrum Principles.*

Scrum Principles

There are six Scrum principles that serve as a basis, or building block, for Scrum. These are mandatory to every project, unlike the aspects and processes that can be modified. You will learn about aspects and processes in the future. The benefits of the principles are realized by the user base of each project, program or portfolio.

The Scrum principles include the following:

1.) Empirical Process Control
2.) Self-Organization
3.) Collaboration
4.) Value-Based Prioritization
5.) Time-Boxing
6.) Iterative Development

We will take a specific look at each principle in the next few days, starting with Empirical Process Control.

DAY 17:

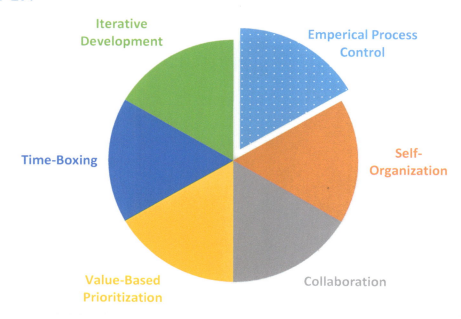

Figure 8: *Empirical Process Control is one of the six Principles of Scrum.*

Empirical Process Control

In terms of Empirical Process Control, there are three key words for you to remember here, and they are as follows:

- *Transparency*
- *Inspection*
- *Adaptation*

These are the important factors of this principle. They refer to the management of Stakeholder expectations, pride of work and ability to make changes along the way. Let's look at each of these words more closely on the next page.

Empirical Process Control (continued)

This will be a little longer topic!

In terms of Empirical Process Control, let's take a deeper dive, starting with Transparency.

Transparency

Transparency is key to management and Stakeholders through artifacts, meetings and what is called <u>INFORMATION RADIATORS</u>. It is necessary that the project is visible and that progress is realized during each and every sprint.

The artifacts include the Project Vision Statement, Prioritized Product Backlog (complete with User Stories) and the Release Planning Schedule (which could be coordinated among several Scrum Teams).

The meetings are the Sprint Review Meetings (which are conducted during the Demonstrate and Validate Sprint process) and Daily Standup Meetings (which are attended by the Scrum Team to discuss daily progress).

The information radiators - Sprint Burndown Chart and Scrumboard.

Notes:

_____
_____
_____
_____
_____
_____

Inspection

Inspection of one's own work and others around is an endless process. This is apparent through use of the following:

- *Scrumboard at Daily Standup Meetings*
- *Frequent and timely feedback through the development of Epics*
- *Creation of the Prioritized Product Backlog*
- *Conducting of Release Planning (determining the product intervals and key dates of release)*
- *And Final Inspection by demonstrating and validating the sprint work*

Adaptation

Adaptation to change through iterative delivery of a product or service happens based on <u>TRANSPARENCY AND INSPECTION</u>. Examples in which adaptation is apparent include the following:

- *Daily Standup Meeting*
- *Retrospect Project Meeting*
- *Retrospect Sprint Meeting*
- *Scrum Guidance Body*
- *Change Requests*
- *And Constant Risk Identification*

And now onto Self-Organization. This term refers to the activity and mindset of the Scrum Team members.

Notes:

_____

_____

_____

_____

_____

Self-Organization

Next is Self-Organization. Since the role of the Scrum Master is to be a servant leader, his or her job is to seek to solve issues and follow up on Scrum Team member's needs. Remember that a Scrum Team that seeks answers and helps others is a Self-Organizing team. This type of structure accepts responsibility and success as a team.

That being said, this type of team also shares expertise, tools and functional knowledge during ALL sprints of a project. For example, at the beginning of the project, they ensure they know what is needed of themselves from a technical standpoint to complete (or develop) the work in Epics and User Stories in the Prioritized Product Backlog. Every single team member of a Scrum Team is to help to determine the length of a sprint, but it is the Product Owner that is responsible for the creation of the User Stories.

As the sprints and project progresses, the Scrum Team attends the Daily Standup Meeting, reprioritizes in the Prioritized Product Backlog Review Meeting, reviews deliverables with Stakeholders and retrospects the lessons learned with the Scrum Master.

The keywords of this principle are as follows:

- *TODAY'S WORKERS as they are able to adapt to changes*
- *SHARED OWNERSHIP since the team owns each feature, not an individual*
- *INNOVATIVE in the applied development approach*
- *WAR ROOM mentality where ideas are shared in the same proximity, often two people to the same computer for idea-sharing*

Next, let's look at Collaboration as we continue through each of the principles of Scrum.

DAY 20:

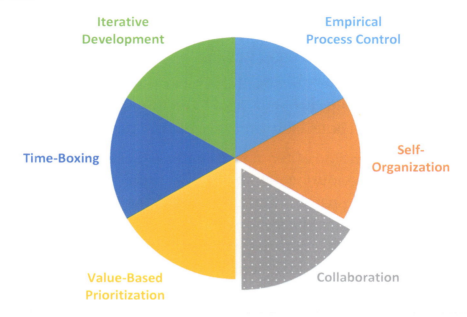

Figure 9: *Collaboration is one of the six Principles of Scrum.*

Collaboration

Continuing around the chart, we have Collaboration. This principle focuses on working seamlessly as a team based on the project vision. During each sprint, the Scrum Team works diligently with Stakeholders to assure value.

That being said, the keywords of this principle are as follows:

- *AWARENESS – the ability to be "in the know" when it comes to the workings and assignments of others on the team*

- *ARTICULATION – the dividing up or separation of work amongst the team members to ensure work is being done in parallel with other features – for the betterment of the project*

- *APPROPRIATION – the use of technology to better one's self*

- *Shared Creation*

The benefits of the Collaboration principle include the following:

- *Risks efficiently identified and mitigated*
- *Poorly specified requirements are lessened*
- *Technical expertise of team is apparent*
- *Constant improvements are assured – giving confidence to the Customer*

The next topic will be Value-Based Prioritization.

You are doing great so far!
We have already covered a good amount of material!

Notes:

_____

_____

_____

_____

_____

_____

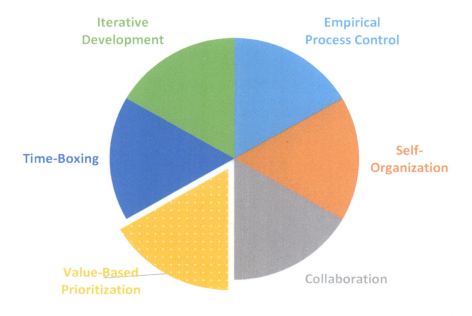

Figure 10: *Value-Based Prioritization is one of the six Principles of Scrum.*

Value-Based Prioritization

The next principle is Value-Based Prioritization. As you might have guessed, this principle focuses on delivering the highest value first.

Prioritization refers to the order of precedence placed on a feature set or story. It determines the necessity an item.

At the time of sprint planning, it is the responsibility of the Product Owner to prioritize the User Stories, after which the Scrum Team estimates effort. The Product Owner must take a look at what it takes to prioritize. There are three factors that go into prioritizing:

- *Value*
- *Risk or Uncertainty*
- *Dependencies*

The keyword of this principle is value or value delivery! Tomorrow we will focus on Time-Boxing.

DAY 22:

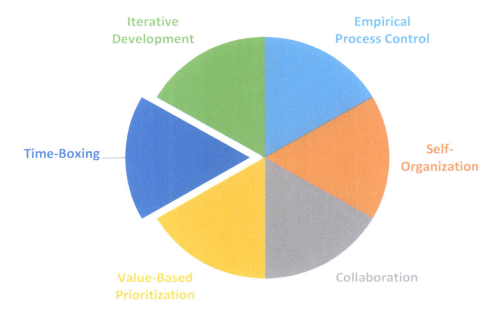

Figure 11: *Time-Boxing is one of the six Principles of Scrum.*

Time-Boxing

Now let's take a look at the idea of time-boxing. Time-Boxing is considered a constraint in Scrum. This has to do with applying a max timeframe to an event of activity. Time-Boxing is done so that the team does not place to much or too little on any portion of a user story, sprint or any part of the project.

There are a few time-boxed activities, sometimes meetings, which are time-boxed that we will detail in a table on the following page.

These are as follows:

- *Short Sprints*
- *Daily Standup Meeting (15 minutes a day)*
- *Sprint Planning Meeting*
- *Sprint Review Meeting*

Time-Boxed Events

This will be a little longer topic!

KEY:

M = Minutes	M = Months	ST = Scrum Team
W = Weeks	PO = Product Owner	
H = Hours	SM = Scrum Master	

MEETING	SHORT SPRINTS	DAILY STANDUP MEETING	SPRINT PLANNING MEETING	SPRINT REVIEW MEETING
DETAIL	1-6 W	15 M	4 H for 2 W Sprint	4 H for 1 M Sprint (same as Retrospect Sprint)
	SM facilitates work; issue mitigation ST creates deliverables PO responsible for value alignment with vision	ST mandatory Often facilitated by SM PO optional Work tracked on Scrumboard based on 3 questions	PO, SM, ST	PO, SM, ST, Executive Sponsors, Customers

Figure 12: A chart showing events that are time-boxed within the Scrum framework.

On the previous page, you can see a table that details several time-boxed Scrum events. The top row gives the name of the activity, and the rows beneath each tells the time frame, participants and more.

The sprints are typically limited to one to six weeks each. These time frames may or may not produce a release of code, but all of them create a potentially shippable increment of functionality or product. The Scrum Master facilitates the work of the Scrum Team as a champion for conflict resolution. Although it is the responsibility of the Scrum Team to share ideas and complete deliverables. During each sprint, the Scrum Team looks at the User Stories, estimates the time involved for each based on the prioritization of the Product Owner. Ultimately, the Product Owner is responsible for business value in alignment with the project vision.

The Daily Standup Meeting is time-boxed to 15 minutes. This meeting is attended by the Scrum Team and often facilitated by the Scrum Master. The Scrum Team is mandatory, whereas, the Product Owner is optional. Work is tracked for transparency on the Scrumboard based on three questions:

- *What did I complete yesterday?*

- *What will I complete today?*

- *What impediments stand in my way?*

The Sprint Planning Meeting is held for four hours per each two-week sprint. It is always at the beginning of the sprint to ensure the right User Stories are assigned to the current sprint. The attendees include the Product Owner, Scrum Master and Scrum Team.

Finally, the Sprint Review Meeting. This meeting is held at the end of the sprint for one to two hours for a two-week sprint. As the name suggests, it is to demo the work of the sprint. The attendees for this meeting include the Product Owner, Scrum Master, Scrum Team, Executive Stakeholders, and possibly, the Customer.

DAY 24:

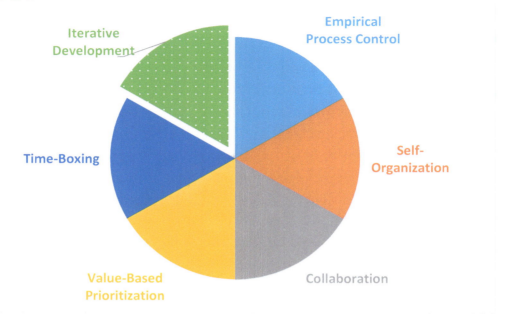

Figure 13: *Iterative Development is one of the six Principles of Scrum.*

Iterative Development

Iterative Development means that the project is developed by the Scrum Team in increments. This ensures a constant and sustainable speed of work that has value to the Customer and is based on the Acceptance Criteria. This type of process allows the Customer to comment, provide feedback and ensure their changes are made to the product along the way.

Throughout the process, User Stories are added to the Prioritized Product Backlog for incorporation in future sprints. During which, the Scrum Master ensures the Scrum ideas are upheld throughout the lifecycle of the project.

Communication and change management are key in this principle.

You are doing great so far!

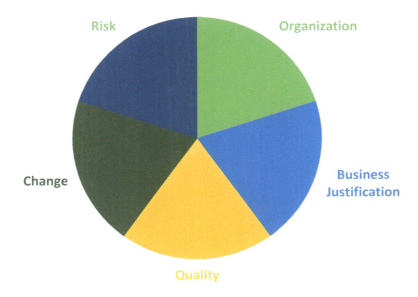

Figure 14: *A chart depicting the five Scrum Aspects.*

Scrum Aspects

There are five Scrum aspects that must be managed and tracked throughout the lifecycle of a Scrum project. These can be modified based on the scope and complexity of the project.

The Scrum aspects include the following:

1. *Organization*

2. *Business Justification*

3. *Quality*

4. *Change*

5. *Risk*

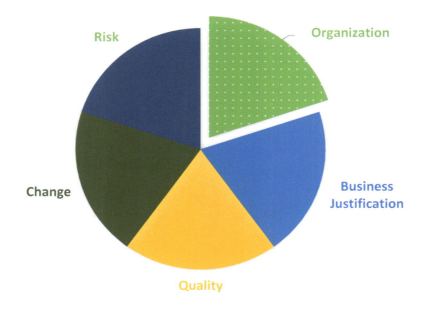

Figure 15: *Organization is one of the five Aspects of Scrum.*

Organization

This information will be a review for you.

Core Roles of Scrum: A Detailed Look

We will begin with the Product Owner – since they typically kickoff the project. This individual is responsible for understanding at a high level, the flow of Scrum as it relates to the Customer <u>AS THE VOICE OF THE CUSTOMER</u>.

While the Scrum Master is a management role, this person is more known as a facilitator. Scrum framework promotes teamwork and team ownership by the clearing of roadblocks or impediments. Notice that there is no position with the title of Project Manager. A Scrum Master is to display a <u>SERVANT LEADER</u> approach.

A Scrum Team typically consists of three to nine people. The team as a whole is responsible for the final implementation of all deliverables.

Non-Core Roles of Scrum: A Detailed Look

The Scrum Guidance Body is typically known as the SGB. This is an optional role and could be a set of documents or a group of combined experts that help in defining objectives regarding quality, government regulations and security. The actual day-to-day work is carried about by the core roles, consisting of the Scrum Team, Scrum Master and Product Owner.

You already know what a Product Owner is, but a Chief Product Owner is a role presiding over multiple Scrum Teams in larger projects. This individual facilitates the work of multiple Product Owners.

A Chief Scrum Master facilitates Scrum activities, just like a single Scrum Team Scrum master, but again, on a larger scale. This role takes a lot of coordination amongst teams.

Stakeholders is sort of a generic term for Users, Customers and Sponsors.

Vendors are the organizations or sometimes even individuals that provide or offer products or services that do <u>NOT</u> fall within the competencies covered by the project.

Each role plays a part in the project, even if not assigned a specific task or item of responsibility.

Notes:

_____

_____

_____

_____

_____

DAY 28:

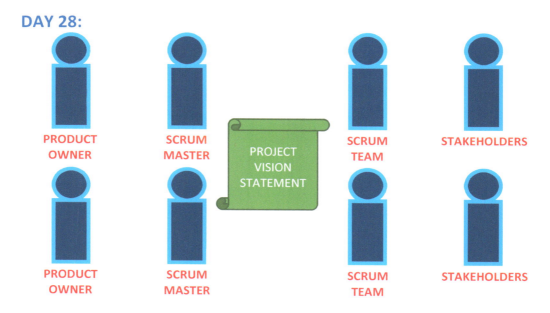

Figure 16: *An illustration of the Scrum project roles in alignment with the Project Vision Statement.*

Project Roles Illustrated

This figure illustrates that <u>ALL</u> roles – both core roles and non-core roles must work together and communicate to achieve project deliverable success based on the Project Vision Statement. No one role is exempt from this process. That is, the Project Vision Statement <u>MUST ALWAYS</u> be at the center of all project work.

Notes:

_____

_____

_____

_____

_____

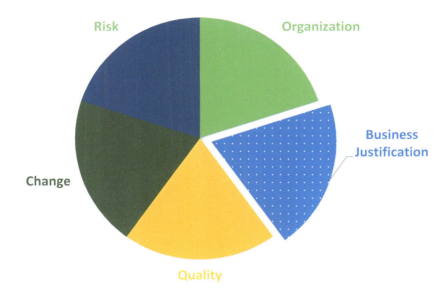

Figure 17: *Business Justification is one of the five Aspects of Scrum.*

Business Justification

Prior to a project kickoff, a Project Business Case must exist. A business case is created to determine the feasibility or existence of the project. At this point, there is no development of work, as even the team members have not yet been selected.

Once the team is in place and work commences, from then until the end of the project – no one person or team member can ever promise project success. The outcome is always uncertain and every person must plan for change – which is <u>ALWAYS</u> inevitable.

Even though change is probable, Quality is still a key. That brings us to the next aspect of Quality.

DAY 30:

Quality

The aspect of Quality speaks to the ability to create themed Epics and User Stories during each sprint according to the Acceptance Criteria.

A <u>THEME</u> is the category that each User Story resides.

An <u>EPIC</u> is a User Story that spans multiple sprints. These are more global in their theming and align with a business culture or organization's core vision.

A <u>USER STORY</u> describes a feature set and is typically inclusive of a persona. That is, they tell from a user's perspective what should happen and what is the benefit.

For example, if the system needs to have a payment portal for external users, then the User Story might be written like this:

"As a buyer, I would like to be able to make payments online in between my typically-scheduled, monthly payment so that I can pay off my account in full at my pace – more efficiently."

Then, a task results when the Scrum Team members look to see what it will take to accomplish such a feature. In the case of our example of the payment portal, a task might be as follows:

"Ensure the portal accepts all major credit card types" or "Create specific login feature for security."

TIP: User Stories may be tracked in a document on an intranet site or on a board – often with sticky notes.

There is a direct relationship between these terms. Tomorrow we will detail this relationship.

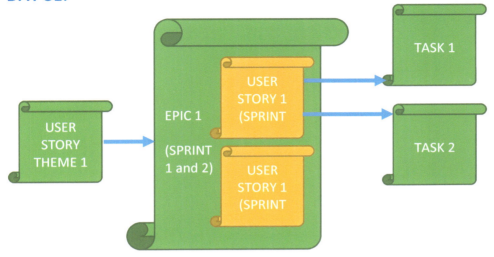

Figure 18: *User Stories, Epics and Tasks Illustrated.*

User Story Relationships

As you can see in this visual illustration, there is a direct relationship between each of the terms learned on the previous page. User Stories typically reside in a single sprint and can contain multiple tasks.

In my experience, I have found that team members tend to use Epic and User Story interchangeably.

Take a moment to view the hierarchy before continuing to the next page about the aspect of Change.

Notes:

_____

_____

_____

_____

_____

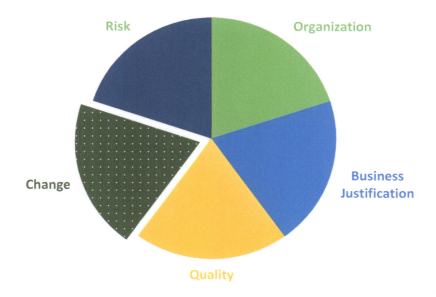

Figure 19: *Change is one of the five Aspects of Scrum.*

Change

The aspect of Change refers to the fact that change is inevitable. Change is something to be planned for and accepted. Throughout the lifecycle of the project, the Customer has a distinct right to change their mind – especially as they see a demo of the product in the Sprint Review Meeting.

Change is managed by short sprint intervals. Customers provide feedback and a change in the course of present action may be needed.

Every change comes with risk. That is, the next aspect is Risk.

You are learning so much information!

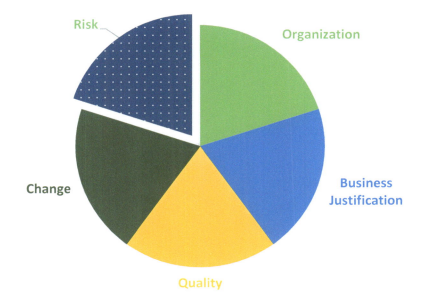

Figure 20: *Risk is one of the five Aspects of Scrum.*

Risk

The last and final aspect is Risk. Risk is defined as uncertainty and will ultimately have either a positive or a negative effect on the project. Positive risks are deemed to be opportunities; whereas, negative risks are called threats.

There are 2 contributing factors that pertain to risk:

1. *Probability of occurrence*

2. *Possible impact of the risk*

Scrum Phases and Processes Overview

PHASES (5)	INITIATE	PLAN and ESTIMATE	IMPLEMENT	REVIEW and RETROSPECT	RELEASE
PROCESSES (19)	Create Project Vision Statement	Create User Stories	Create Deliverable	Convene Scrum of Scrums	Ship Deliverables
	Identify Scrum Master and Stakeholders	Approve, Estimate and Commit User Stories	Conduct Daily Standup Meeting	Demonstrate and Validate Sprint	Retrospect Project
	Form Scrum Team	Create Tasks	Groom (Update) Prioritized Product Backlog	Retrospect Sprint	
	Develop Epics	Estimate Tasks			
	Create Prioritized Product Backlog	Create Sprint Backlog			
	Conduct Release Planning				

Figure 21: *Processes and Phases Overview.*

Keep up the good work to date!

Pictured on the previous page are the five Phases and 19 Processes of Scrum.

TIP: It is essential for nearly every Scrum exam to have a firm foundation of what processes fall within each phase of a Scrum project. Therefore, we will spend a significant amount of time talking about each of these processes, by phase, as well as the INPUTS, TOOLS and OUTPUTS.

Looking at the table, the first phase is Initiate. In the Initiate phase, you have six processes:

- *Create Project Vision Statement*
- *Identify Scrum Master and Stakeholders*
- *Form Scrum Team*
- *Develop Epics*
- *Create Prioritized Product Backlog*
- *Conduct Release Planning*

Some of these topics we have already covered; whereas, others we will detail for you in the coming pages. Each of the phases will be represented by a new table in a unique phase color. You will see that some of the details span multiple processes, do not be alarmed. Simply know where that piece of information fits into the big picture. Oftentimes the output of one process ends up being the input of one or more following processes.

Throughout the phases, we have tried to distribute the amount of information to avoid information overload.

DAY 35:

INITIATE	INPUTS		TOOLS		OUTPUTS	
Create Project Vision Statement	Project Business Case	*	Project Vision Meeting	*	Identified Product Owner	*
	Program Product Owner		JAD Sessions		Project Vision Statement	*
	Program Scrum Master		SWOT Analysis		Project Charter	
	Program Stakeholders		Gap Analysis		Project Budget	
	Chief Product Owner					
	Program Product Backlog					
	Trial Project					
	Proof of Concept					
	Company Vision					
	Market Study					
	Scrum Guidance Body Recommendations					

Figure 22: *The Inputs, Tools and Outputs for the Create Project Vision Statement Process in the Initiate Phase.*

Create Project Vision Statement

This is a process of the Initiate phase.

This topic has...you guessed it....another table. Notice that the first process in the Initiate phase is in the left-most column. The second column shows the Inputs, or what it takes to achieve the Outputs of the process. I am going to ignore the columns with the asterisks at this point. Continuing to the right, you can see the Tools or 'vehicles' needed to complete the process. Finally, the Outputs are the results of the process completion.

Now, there are several items in this table that have an asterisks (*) to the right. Those items are mandatory to the process of create Project Vision Statement. You now know how to read this type of table, now let's detail the content.

You know how to define the Project Vision Statement, but this visual provides an illustration of the things, events or artifacts that go into creating the Project Vision Statement. For example, the Project Business Case must be in place prior to creating the Project Vision Statement. That is, you have to justify the project's existence before you can kick off the project and have a direction.

Notes:

_____

_____

_____

_____

_____

Create Project Vision Statement (continued)

Likewise, the Scrum Master, Chief Product Owner and possibly the Product Owner should be in place prior to the team member selection.

Additionally, a Market Study should be completed to determine the feasibility and the general, high-level requirements determined at this point.

Finally, you have to have the Scrum Guidance Body available as guidance from the very start.

The Tools, such as the Project Vision Meeting, JAD Sessions, SWOT Analysis and Gap Analysis are all ways to help you come up with vision, requirements, charter, budget and so on.

Do not be intimidated by new words or definitions, the previous table is simply a roadmap. Over the coming pages, we will take a closer look to fill in the gaps.

The next topic we will discuss Business Justification.

Notes:

_____

_____

_____

_____

_____

Business Justification

There are several tools and calculations to be used to determine the value of a project. Some of the common tools include the following:

1. *RIO Calculation, which takes the project expected revenue and subtracts the project expected investment costs to come up with the net profit, then divides that figure by the project expected investment costs to equal the rate of return. This calculation is affected by interest rates as well as inflation dollars.*

2. **ACR** *NPV stands for Net Present Value is the total sum of the Present Value (PV) of cash flow (cash in and cash out) over a specified time frame. In other words, a higher NPV is optimal.*

3. **ACR** *IRR stands for Internal Rate of Return and it is a method of calculating rate of return. The term internal means that it does <u>NOT</u> incorporate outside, such as interest rates or inflation dollars.*

Now let's look at the Proof of Project, where the visualization of the end product begins.

Notes:

_____

_____

_____

_____

_____

DAY 38:

INITIATE	INPUTS
Create Project Vision Statement	Project Business Case *
	Program Product Owner
	Program Scrum Master
	Program Stakeholders
	Chief Product Owner
	Program Product Backlog
	Trial Project
	Proof of Concept
	Company Vision
	Market Study
	Scrum Guidance Body Recommendations

Figure 23: *Trial Project and Proof of Concept are both Inputs to the Create Project Vision Statement Process in the Initiate Phase.*

Trial Project or Proof of Concept

This is an input to the Create Project Vision process in the Initiate phase.

It generally refers to a visual or a portion being created during an initial sprint or portion of a sprint. This is to give end users an idea or glimpse of what is to come. It is not the full list of requirements stuffed into a really short amount of time, but a foreshadowing of what the full end result *could* look like.

Continuing along, let's take a peek at JAD Sessions.

You are doing AMAZING!

DAY 39:

TOOLS

Project Vision Meeting   *

JAD Sessions

SWOT Analysis

Gap Analysis

Figure 24: JAD Sessions is a Tool for the Create Project Vision Statement Process in the Initiate Phase.

JAD Sessions

This is a tool for the Create Project Vision Statement process in the Initiate phase.

ACR *JAD stands for Joint Application Design.* It is a requirements gathering meeting or workshop that takes place with users to better understand what is needed to develop the feature set. The benefits of this meeting include:

- *Greater participation from users throughout the lifecycle of the project as a result*
- *Efficient development due to clarified requirements*
- *Quality specifications transparent to all team members*

And now onto SWOT Analysis.

Notes:

_____

_____

_____

_____

_____

Sᴛʀᴇɴɢᴛʜs	Wᴇᴀᴋɴᴇssᴇs
Oᴘᴘᴏʀᴛᴜɴɪᴛɪᴇs	Tʜʀᴇᴀᴛs

Figure 25: *SWOT Analysis is an acronym as shown in this illustration.*

SWOT Analysis

This too is a tool for the Create Project Vision Statement process in the Initiate phase.

ACR SWOT is an acronym and is a method for initial planning or decision making for a project, product or service through identification of strengths, weaknesses, opportunities and threats.

- *S stands for Strengths*
- *W for Weaknesses*
- *for Opportunities*
- *T for Threats*

Keep in mind that Strengths and Weaknesses are internal factors by where the resources are constantly available and Opportunities and Threats are outside factors in which you often to <u>NOT</u> have any control.

TIP: All these factors combined help the team identify impacts for the project. Be sure to know what the acronym stands for.

Now let's take a brief look at Gap Analysis.

DAY 41:

TOOLS

Project Vision Meeting   *

JAD Sessions

SWOT Analysis

Gap Analysis

Figure 26: GAP Analysis is a Tool for the Create Project Vision Statement Process in the Initiate Phase.

Gap Analysis

This is another tool for the Create Project Vision Statement process in the Initiate phase.

Gap analysis is a technique that involves the comparison of current state with the future or ideal state of a business in order to improve processes across a project or organization.

The Gap Analysis highlights inefficiencies so business can be run at an optimal level for the best chances of success.

In the next topic, we will compare the Prioritized Product Backlog to the Sprint Backlog.

Notes:

_____

_____

_____

_____

_____

DAY 42:

Figure 27: *Items in the Sprint Backlog ultimately come from the Prioritized Product Backlog.*

Prioritized Product Backlog versus Sprint Backlog

The items in the Prioritized Product Backlog are added by the Product Owner with input from the Scrum Team. These items are added after much communication with the Stakeholders so they know and understand what is most valuable to the Customer. These item or User Stories are listed here for the entire project and can be broken down as needed. The breaking down of this information is called <u>DECOMPOSITION</u>.

The items are each given a persona, or a role to better picture who will use the feature being developed, how they will use it and to what benefit that person will have once the feature is made available. The stories are assigned Acceptance Criteria that will be used later in the sprint in the Sprint Review Meeting to help the Product Owner decide if the User Stories and tasks meet the criteria to be approved and done.

Once the list of User Stories is devised, the highest priority items are added to the top of the list. Then, the Sprint Planning Meeting is used to look at the top of the list. The Scrum Team estimates the top features and the items are assigned to the current sprint. The Sprint Backlog holds the individual tasks that it will take to complete the User Stories.

DAY 43:

OUTPUTS	
Identified Product Owner	*

Project Vision Statement	*
Project Charter	
Project Budget	

Figure 28: *Project Vision Statement is an Output for the Create Project Vision Statement Process in the Initiate Phase.*

Project Vision Statement

This is an output for the Create Project Vision Statement process in the Initiate phase.

In review, The Project Vision Statement is an output of the Create Project Vision process. It explains the business need for a project and is typically a document that is visible to all Stakeholders as well as the Scrum Team. The details serve as a firm foundation for every project activity or event.

Next, the Project Vision Statement will be crafted explaining the goals of the project. At this point, the team is starting to take shape as the vision is being formed.

Notes:

_____

_____

_____

_____

_____

DAY 44:

INITIATE	INPUTS		TOOLS		OUTPUTS	
Identify Scrum Master and Stakeholders	Product Owner	*	Selection Criteria	*	Identified Scrum Master	*
	Project Vision Statement	*	Expert Advice from HR		Identified Stakeholders	*
	Program Product Owner		Training and Costs			
	Program Scrum Master		Resource Costs			
	Chief Product Owner					
	Chief Scrum Master					
	Program Stakeholders					
	People Requirements					
	People Availability and Commitment					
	Org Resource Matrix					
	Skills Requirement Matrix					
	Scrum Guidance Body Recommendations					

Figure 29: A chart showing the Inputs, Tools and Outputs of the Identify Scrum Master and Stakeholders Process in the Initiate Phase.

Identify Scrum Master and Stakeholders

This is a process of the Initiate phase.

Once the project vision is in place, the Scrum Team members are identified. Just as before, the Inputs column shows what it takes to make this happen, the Tools help you get there and the Outputs are the results of this process.

Notice that the Product Owner is typically in place prior to the Scrum Master and Scrum Team.

Likewise, the requirements must be defined, at a high-level, and the SGB, so that when the Scrum Team <u>IS</u> in place, they know the direction to which to head.

ACR   The selection criteria along with advice from *HR (Human Resources)* make it possible to get the team in place and in-house. As always, there is a time of training and transition that lead to the best decisions in terms of the talents on the team.

We will now review the SGB.

TIP: Repetition is the name of the game when it comes to not only passing Scrum exams, but also being able to apply the concepts in real, everyday life.

Notes:

———————————————————————————————

———————————————————————————————

———————————————————————————————

———————————————————————————————

———————————————————————————————

DAY 45:

INITIATE	INPUTS	
Identify Scrum Master and Stakeholders	Product Owner	*
	Project Vision Statement	*
	Program Product Owner	
	Program Scrum Master	
	Chief Product Owner	
	Chief Scrum Master	
	Program Stakeholders	
	People Requirements	
	People Availability and Commitment	
	Org Resource Matrix	
	Skills Requirement Matrix	
	Scrum Guidance Body Recommendations	

Figure 30: *Scrum Guidance Body Recommendations is an Input of the Identify Scrum Master and Stakeholders Process in the Initiate Phase.*

Scrum Guidance Body

This is an input of the Identify Scrum Master and Stakeholders process in the Initiate phase.

ACR The *Scrum Guidance Body is typically known as the SGB* – we mentioned this in the past, but it never hurts to read the details again.

The SGB is an optional role and could be a set of documents or a group of combined experts that help in defining objectives regarding quality, government regulations and security. If the SGB is a group of experts, these individuals DO NOT make decisions for the project.

The actual day-to-day work is carried about by the core roles, consisting of the Scrum Team, Scrum Master and Product Owner.

DAY 46:

INITIATE	INPUTS		TOOLS		OUTPUTS	
Form Scrum Team	Product Owner	*	Scrum Team Selection	*	Identified Scrum Team	*
	Scrum Master	*	Expert Advice from HR		Backup Persons	
	Project Vision Statement		People Costs		Collaboration Plan	
	Chief Product Owner		Training and Costs		Team Building Plan	
	People Requirements		Resource Costs			
	People Availability and Commitment					
	Organizational Resource Matrix					
	Skills Requirement Matrix					
	Resource Requirements					
	Scrum Guidance Body Recommendations					

Figure 31: A chart showing the Inputs, Tools and Outputs of the Form Scrum Team Process in the Initiate Phase.

Form Scrum Team

When a Scrum Team is newly formed, you know that there is a lot that goes into each decision. The ultimate decisions regarding the project developers belongs to the Product Owner – sometimes alongside the Scrum Master. The list of Inputs to this process is lengthy, but worth the time investment to get the right people for the right job based on the right selection criteria! An effective team, big picture, MUST be highly collaborative with all levels of the organization!

Even though these individuals are highly-skilled and cross-functional, it is important to have a backup plan for each type of knowledge or skill set.

For example, if Bobby is a Scrum Team member and he is an expert at creating an online payment portal, it is important that as time allows, he trains another team member to have a similar skill set. Both inside influences, such as management and outside challenges, such as Bobby becoming sick could impact the deliverables and the sprint timeline unless his skills can be covered by an alternative person on the team.

On the previous page, you can see that in order to form the Scrum Team, you must have the right training tools and resources available to make the team successful.

On the next page, we will delve into the shaping of a new Scrum Team and the process that each new team seems to employ.

DAY 47:

The Shaping of a New Scrum Team

Tuckman's Model of Group Dynamics states that a new Scrum Team evolves from its infancy to a fully, well-working team. This new team goes through stages beginning with Forming and ending with Performing.

In the Forming stage, this is a new and exciting stage for the team because everything is new, few impediments and struggles have yet to exist.

The next stage in this model is Storming. It is during this stage that challenges tend to arise. The team members may have disagreements and want to overpower each other. Power struggles between members may exist making this stage a challenge.

The following stage is Norming, by where the team members of a Scrum Team, particularly a newly-formed Scrum Team begins to become an experienced Scrum Team. This takes a time frame of getting used to the potentially new structure and order of activities. Sharing is likely to take place, and they are more likely to work together as a cohesive team.

The final team stage is Performing. In this last and final phase, the team works, functions and <u>PERFORMS</u> at their peak. Efficiencies are in place and repeatable practices.

Notes:

_____

_____

_____

_____

_____

INITIATE	INPUTS		TOOLS		OUTPUTS	
Develop Epics	Scrum Core Team	*	User Group Meetings	*	Epics	*
	Project Vision Statement	*	User Story Workshops		Personas	*
	Stakeholders		Focus Group Meetings		Approved Changes	
	Program Product Log		User or Customer Interviews		Identified Risks	
	Approved Change Requests		Questionnaires			
	Unapproved Change Requests		Risk Identification Techniques			
	Program and Portfolio Risks		Scrum Guidance Body Expertise			
	Laws and Regulations					
	Applicable Contracts					
	Previous Project Information					
	Scrum Guidance Body Recommendations					

Figure 32: *A chart showing the Inputs, Tools and Outputs of the Develop Epics Process in the Initiate Phase.*

Develop Epics

This is a process in the Initiate phase.

In this process, user Group Meetings are held to develop Epics based on the Project Vision Statement. Epics help determine the course of action for development and lessen project risk.

During the development of Epics, changes (in the form of Change Requests) may be needed and risks identified.

The next topic is Change Request and the tracking of changes.

*You are well on your way
to YOUR professional success!*

Notes:

_____

_____

_____

_____

_____

DAY 49:

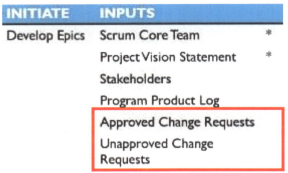

Figure 33: *Approved and Unapproved Change Requests are Inputs for the Develop Epics Process in the Initiate Phase.*

Change Requests

Approved and Unapproved Change Requests are both inputs of the Develop Epics process in the Initiate Phase.

You already know that change in every project is unavoidable. Change Requests are documented, suggested changes from the original requirements that come from any role in the project or organization. Change Requests remain in a state of Unapproved until approved in a formal process. Typically the Scrum Guidance Body outlines a formal process of Change Request approval.

When a formal approval process is <u>NOT</u> in place, the Product Owner is able to approve changes that are small in scope. The determination of what classifies as small ultimately falls upon senior management. Some changes require senior management.

Once a Change Request is approved, the change is added to the Prioritized Product Backlog for prioritization in a future sprint.

Change Requests are not only discussed in the Develop Epics process, but also during the Create Prioritized Product Backlog and Groom (Update) Prioritized Product Backlog processes.

Finally, let's look at identifying risk. Like change, risk happens at all points in the lifecycle in projects, programs and portfolios.

DAY 50:

Risks Overview

Risks are events that are unpredictable in nature that <u>COULD</u> affect the <u>FUTURE</u> state of the project in either a positive way or a negative way. Positive risk or success is called opportunity. Whereas, negative or failure is called a threat. Risk as a whole is managed iteratively throughout the project lifecycle. It is important to be able to pick out an example of risk from a list of options. One such example might be as follows:

The construction project timeline for a new golf club house could experience delay due to the impending hurricane in the gulf. That is an outside risk.

There are three buckets or categories with regard to risk:

1. *Identification*

2. *Assessment*

3. *Prioritization*

TIP: *Risk that is not addressed is likely to become an issue. That phrase is worth repeating – so - Risk that is not addressed is likely to become an issue.*

Next, let's look into several available risk identification techniques.

Notes:

_____

_____

_____

_____

_____

DAY 51:

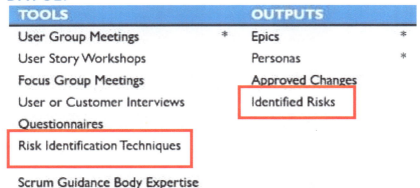

Figure 34: *Risk Identification is a Tool and Identified Risks is an Output of the Develop Epics Process of the Initiate Phase.*

Risk Identification

There are several tools used in identifying risk. These options are:

1. *Reviewing the outcomes previous Retrospect Sprint Meetings or Retrospect Project Meetings in terms of the successes, improvements needed and/or actions to be taken.*

2. *Risk Checklist – lists the common encounters by category*

3. *Risk Prompt List – for coming up with the source of risk*

4. *Brainstorming – to promote idea sharing between members and a facilitator*

5. ***ACR*** *RBS – stands for Risk Breakdown Structure – which is a grouping of risk to find types or common theming*

6. *And Risk-Based Spike – which is a two to three day event or experiment at the beginning of the project (prior to the development of Epics) with research and possibly even prototyping to better understand the potential for risk*

Once risk is identified, is MUST be assessed. Let's look at risk assessment next.

DAY 52:

Risk Assessment

ACR Risk assessment is defined as analysis of the probability of occurrence and net effect on a project or organization. These effects can be analyzed using risk models and by measuring *EMV or Expected Monetary Value.*

We will mention 4 of the risk models in brief detail here:

1. *Risk Meeting – a meeting by where core Scrum Team members convene to prioritize risk – Stakeholders are optional attendees*

2. *Probability Tree – where possible events are presented in a tree-like shape by where the branches are extended for each possible outcome*

3. *Pareto Analysis – a chart showing risk ranked for impact showing the 80/20 rule – where 20 % of the risks typically make up 80 % of the impact*

4. *Probability Impact Grid – this is a visual that uses the following calculation: Probability x Impact = Severity – where probability and Impact are both assigned a scale independent of each other, such as decimal ranges or whole number ranges*

And finally, EMV, which as you know stands for Expected Monetary Value, calculates the monetary value of a risk. The calculation is as follows: EMV = NEGATIVE Risk Impact ($) x Risk Probability OCCURRENCE (%).

To finish off the topic of risks, we will end with risk prioritization.

DAY 53:

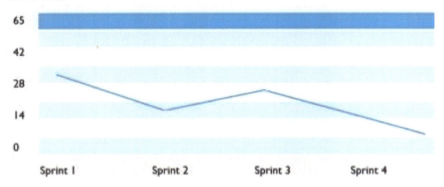

Figure 35: *Risk Prioritization in a charted illustration.*

Risk Prioritization

Risks can be ranked after identification and assessment is complete. Risk prioritization involves ranking or putting an order to the risks identified.

Overall, risk can be mitigated through regular feedback, continued flexibility, complete transparency and iterative development.

Risk should be visible to all and communicated. An important tool or chart used to communicate risk is the Risk Burndown Chart, which depicts the likelihood of occurrence of specific risks across all sprints.

The terms risks and issues are often used interchangeably; therefore, let's spend just a brief moment looking at issues.

Notes:

_____

_____

_____

_____

_____

DAY 54:

Issues

Issues are often confused with risk. Issues are certain and deal with the current moment versus the future, as in risk.

An example of an issue is as follows:

"The deployment of a needed, outside development tool that was delayed."

Keep up the positive momentum!

Notes:

_____

_____

_____

_____

_____

DAY 55:

INITIATE	INPUTS		TOOLS		OUTPUTS	
Create Prioritized Product Backlog	Scrum Core Team	*	User Story Prioritization	*	Prioritized Product Backlog	*
	Epics	*	User Story Workshops		Done Criteria	*
	Personas	*	Planning for Value			
	Stakeholders		Risk Assessment Techniques			
	Project Vision Statement		Estimation of Project Value			
	Program Product Backlog		User Story Estimation Methods			
	Business Requirements		Scrum Guidance body Expertise			
	Approved Change Requests					
	Identified Risks					
	Applicable Contracts					
	Scrum Guidance Body Recommendations					

Figure 36: *A chart showing the Inputs, Tools and Outputs for the Create Prioritized Product Backlog Process in the Initiate Phase.*

Create Prioritized Product Backlog

This is a process in the Initiate phase.

In this process Epics are modified and prioritized to create the Prioritized Product Backlog for the duration of the project. Done Criteria is also established as an outcome or Output.

Let's elaborate on User Story Methodology next.

Notes:

_____

_____

_____

_____

_____

KNOWLEDGE ASSESSMENT:

An important tool or chart used to measure risk is the

_____.

    A. User Story Chart
    B. Burndown Chart
    C. Estimation Chart
    D. Value-Gained Chart

Figure 37: *Bill Wake talked about INVEST as a User Story acronym.*

User Stories

These are discussed and referenced throughout the Scrum lifecycle.

ACR   Each user story is to follow the Invest Method. Bill Wake talked about INVEST being an acronym for the characteristics each user story should possess. Remember that when the Scrum Team or development team go to develop the work done for each task, there is always a testing function, either by the same person or a different person of the team that must test that block of functionality. The testing must be able to be done for the isolated feature as well as how that feature plays into the big project picture.

Therefore, the story must be able to stand alone or be *independent*.

Each should be *negotiable* in that they are changeable, rewritten.

They should also be *valuable* – benefits to the Customer?

The team members should be able to *estimate* the work effort needed and divide it into tasks.

Next, they should be *small* enough to be divided and fit into a sprint.

Finally, they need to be *testable*. The job of any developer is to look at ways of refactoring the code for ease of readability.

Now that we have defined and given you the method of user stories, let's take a peek at prioritization methods.

DAY 57:

MoSCoW	Simple Schemes	Monopoly Money
Labels in descending order	Labeling simplified like 1, 2, 3 or H,M,L	Customers given FAKE money representing total project budget
Acronym: -Must Have (no value without) -Should Have -Could Have -Won't Have (not included)	Tends to have too many HIGHs	Looks at what the customer is willing to PAY for a story

Figure 38: *User Story Prioritization Methods (Part 1).*

Paired Comparison	100-Point Method	Kano Analysis
Two user stories are paired against the other	Developed by Dean Leffingwell and Don Widrig	Developed by Noriaki Kano
The "winner" of the two receives the higher value	Customer given 100 points to use in all for any user stories – at the end – all points for each story from each user is tallied to prioritize	Requirements classification into four Categories: -Exciters/Delighters -Satisfiers -Dissatisfiers -Indifferent

Figure 39: *User Story Prioritization Methods (Part 2).*

User Story Prioritization Methods

This will be a little longer topic!

There are six User Story Prioritization Methods we will look at for assigning value to the items in the Prioritized Product Backlog:

1. **ACR** *MoSCoW – notice the lettering; this is also an acronym using the capitalized letters:*

   1. *Must Have*

   2. *Should Have*

   3. *Could Have*

   4. *Won't Have*

      a. *These labels are in descending order left to right...in this method, users are asked which "bucket" they fall into.*

2. *Simple Schemes – which involves the use of similar reasoning, but a simple numbering scheme or clothing sizes – the challenge with this method is that it is easy to give all stories the top values or high values.*

3. *Monopoly Money – involves giving the Customers or attendees fake money equaling the project budget so you can see what they are willing to pay for specific features.*

4. *Paired Comparison – is where you compare one story to another and determine the value of each when looked at together.*

5. *100-Point Method – is when you give each person 100 points and tell each user to "spend" them how they see fit – the story with the highest points received the highest value or priority.*

6. And finally, Kano Analysis – requires classification into four categories:

    1. Exciters and Delighters – which are determined to be features with the highest values to the Customer.

    2. Satisfiers – which are features that add value to the Customer.

    3. Dissatisfiers – are features that if <u>NOT</u> present, the Customer will dislike the product, but do not affect the satisfaction levels if present.

    4. Indifferent – features that do not affect the Customer in any way and should be eliminated.

You are well on your way to overall project success!

Notes:

_____

_____

_____

_____

_____

INITIATE	INPUTS		TOOLS		OUTPUTS	
Conduct Release Planning	Scrum Core Team	*	Release Planning Sessions	*	Release Planning Schedule	*
	Stakeholders		Release Prioritization Methods	*	Length of Sprint	*
	Project Vision Statement	*			Target Customers	
	Prioritized Product Backlog	*			Refined Prioritized Product Backlog	
	Done Criteria	*				
	Program Product Owner					
	Program Scrum Master					
	Chief Product Owner					
	Program Product Backlog					
	Business Reqs.					
	Holiday Calendar					
	Scrum Guidance Body Recommendations					

Figure 40: A chart showing the Inputs, Tools and Outputs for the Conduct Release Planning Process in the Initiate Phase.

Conduct Release Planning

This is a process in the Initiate phase.

For this process, the Scrum Team reviews the highest level stories and creates the Release Planning Schedule. This outlines the deployments schedule in each phase of the project lifecycle. This is a documentation of the milestones, release dates, sprint dates, meetings and the length of the sprints that can be shared with the Stakeholders for total visibility.

Notice that conducting the release planning is not unlike any other time you plan a big event or project of any type – you have to take into account team member vacation schedules, calendar holidays and any corporate initiatives that might affect the timeline.

One of the Inputs that we have only briefly talked on to this point is Done Criteria. Let's look at this on the next page.

KNOWLEDGE ASSESSMENT:

According to Kano Analysis, _____ are determined to be features with the highest values to the Customers.

    A. Exciters/Delighters
    B. Satisfiers
    C. Dissatisfiers
    D. Indifferent

DAY 59:

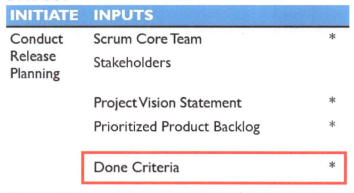

INITIATE	INPUTS	
Conduct Release Planning	Scrum Core Team	*
	Stakeholders	
	Project Vision Statement	*
	Prioritized Product Backlog	*
	Done Criteria	*

Figure 41: *Done Criteria is an Input for the Conduct Release Planning Process in the Initiate Phase.*

Done Criteria

This is an Input for the Conduct Release Planning process of the Initiate phase.

Each Scrum Team has their own definition of Done Criteria or Acceptance Criteria for all User Stories. The definition of done determines if a User Story was successfully completed.

During the Sprint Review Meeting, the Scrum Master or Scrum Team provides the Stakeholders with a demo. During which the Product Owner determines if the item is marked as done and can potentially be shipped to the Customer OR if the User Story is added back to the Prioritized Product Backlog for inclusion in a future sprint.

Notes:

_____

_____

_____

_____

_____

PLAN and ESTIMATE	INPUTS		TOOLS		OUTPUTS	
Create User Stories	Scrum Core Team	*	User Story Writing Expertise	*	User Stories	*
	Prioritized Product Backlog	*	User Story Workshops		User Story Acceptance Criteria	*
	Done Criteria	*	User Group Meetings		Updated Prioritized Product Backlog	
	Personas	*	Focus Group Meetings			
	Stakeholders		Customer or User Interviews			
	Epics		Questionnaires			
	Business Requirements		User Story Estimation Methods			
	Laws and Regulations		Scrum Guidance Body Expertise			
	Applicable Contracts					
	Scrum Guidance Body Recommendations					

Figure 42: A chart showing the Inputs, Tools and Outputs for the Create User Stories Process in the Plan and Estimate Phase.

Create User Stories

This is a process in the Plan and Estimate phase.

During this phase, user stories and the applicable Acceptance Criteria are created. The User Stories are typically written initially by the Product Owner, but then the Scrum Team refines the list. All in all. User Stories are prioritized into the sprints of the project.

As you can see in the diagram on the previous page, there are several Inputs, such as the creation of personas or persons, business requirements, contracts and SGB that go into the creation. Tools such as User Story Workshops, interviews with Customers and questionnaires help you to arrive at Committed User Stories and the refinements of the items in the Prioritized Product Backlog.

Let's take a specific look next at the User Story Workshops.

Notes:

_____

_____

_____

_____

_____

DAY 61:

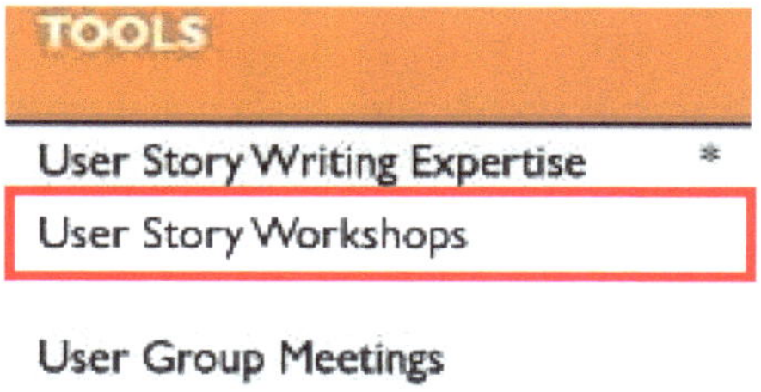

TOOLS
User Story Writing Expertise   *
User Story Workshops

User Group Meetings

Figure 43: Use Story Workshops is a Tool for the Create User Stories Process in the Plan and Estimate Phase.

User Story Workshops

This is a tool for the Create User Stories process of the Plan and Estimate phase.

These are held as part of the Develop Epics Process and are facilitated by the Scrum Master. The Scrum Team is involved and maybe the Stakeholders too. This type of meeting tends to assist the Product Owner in the prioritization of requirements. It helps to ensure the Users Stories are written with personas from a user's standpoint.

The main goal of the User Story Workshop is to get a grasp on the expectations of each deliverable.

Notes:

_____

_____

_____

_____

_____

PLAN and ESTIMATE	INPUTS		TOOLS		OUTPUTS	
Approve, Estimate and Commit User Stories	Scrum Core Team	*	User Group Meetings	*	Approved, Estimated and Committed User Stories	*
	User Stories	*	Planning Poker			
	User Story Acceptance Criteria	*	Fist of Five			
	Scrum Guidance Body Recommendations		Points for Cost Estimation			
			Other Estimation Techniques			
			Scrum Guidance Body Expertise			

Figure 44: *A chart showing the Inputs, Tools and Outputs for the Approve, Estimate and Commit User Stories Process in the Plan and Estimate Phase.*

Approve, Estimate and Commit User Stories

This is a process of the Plan and Estimate phase. During this process, the Product Owner approves stories that have been committed to a sprint. The Scrum Master and Scrum Team estimate the effort required for features. The Scrum Team commits to deliver features according to the highest value to form the Approved, Estimated and Committed User Stories. We will take a look at some of the tools:

- *User Group Meetings*
- *Planning Poker*
- *Fist of Five*

DAY 63:

TOOLS
User Group Meetings   *

Planning Poker

Fist of Five

Figure 45: User Group Meetings is a Tool for the Approve, Estimate and Commit User Stories Process in the Plan and Estimate Phase.

User Group Meetings

One of the tools in the Approve, Estimate and Commit User Stories is User Group Meetings - also referred to as Task Planning Meetings.

These are meetings with Stakeholders or users to create a common understanding of the requirements for task completion, formulate Acceptance Criteria for user stories and to create a sense of confidence with this group that the developers now know how to proceed with development efforts.

Let's look at another tool to this process, Planning Poker.

KNOWLEDGE ASSESSMENT:

Which of the following User Story prioritization methods involves giving customers face money equaling the project budget?

A. Paired Comparison
B. Monopoly Money
C. 100-Point Method
D. None of the Above

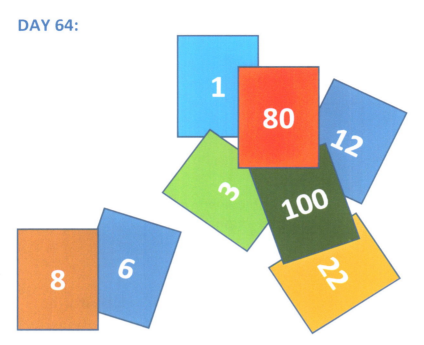

Figure 46: Planning Poker is also called Scrum Poker.

Planning Poker

Planning Poker is also called Scrum Poker. It is a technique for estimating the effort needed in the creation of User Stories.

The Scrum Master reads a story or statement and the Scrum Team members use the numbered cards to state their estimation or value, in their opinion. Each team member listens as the statement is read, then votes by placing the value it best represents face down on the table so others cannot see how they voted. Then each person is asked to turn over their card. The outliers explain why they voted out of norm. Revoting happens until a consensus is reached.

Something to note for your exams is that it is a variation of the Wideband Delphi Method which is also based on a team consensus.

And now onto an additional tool in the Approve, Estimate and Commit User Story process is Fist of Fives.

Fist of Fives

This is a decision-making technique used when the team lacks confidence in a team decision, such as User Story prioritization. It is an option based on consensus by a use of fingers in the air. This method is a voting-styled approach. Each person essentially votes after hearing the statement by using their hands. Each person casts their vote and then explains why they voted the way that they did. The five voting options are as follows:

- *5 – Disagrees with the group decision with major concerns*
- *4 – Disagrees with the group decision with minor concerns*
- *3 – Not sure of response, but willing to go with group decision*
- *2 – Agrees with the group decision with minor concerns*
- *1 – Agrees with the group decision with major concerns*

TIP: REMEMBER...the concept of team ownership in Scrum is a very important concept to remember. So the team has to 'live' with the consensus as a team!

Lots of groundwork has already been covered!

Notes:

_____

_____

_____

_____

_____

PLAN and ESTIMATE	INPUTS		TOOLS		OUTPUTS	
Create Tasks	Scrum Core Team	*	Task Planning Meetings	*	Task List	*
	Approved, Estimated and Committed User Stories	*	Index Cards		Updated, Approved, Estimated and Committed User Stories	
			Decomposition		Dependencies	
			Dependency Determination			

Figure 47: *A chart showing the Inputs, Tools and Outputs for the Create Tasks Process in the Plan and Estimate Phase.*

Create Tasks

This a process in the Plan and Estimate phase.

During this process, the approved, estimated and committed User Stories are broken down into smaller, more manageable chunks called tasks. The entire list of tasks is called the Task List. In order to devise the total list of tasks, a Tool called the Task Planning Meeting takes place.

Index Cards are also a helpful tool in aiding the team in the visualization of the big picture by allowing attendees to write on cards, during brainstorming, and add them to the board in a portable and changeable manner.

Let's take a look at the uses of index cards in the creation of many artifacts of Scrum, including tasks.

DAY 67:

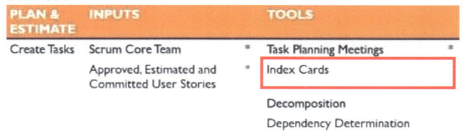

PLAN & ESTIMATE	INPUTS		TOOLS	
Create Tasks	Scrum Core Team	*	Task Planning Meetings	*
	Approved, Estimated and Committed User Stories	*	Index Cards	
			Decomposition	
			Dependency Determination	

Figure 48: *Index Cards is a Tool for the Create Tasks Process in the Plan and Estimate Phase.*

Index Cards

Index Cards are tool of the Create Tasks process in the Plan and Estimate phase. These are exactly what you think they are – little 3x5 or so cards that are low-tech, inexpensive to buy and easy to carry around from room to room. Index Cards are helpful when planning the release or the sprint. For instance, the Product Owner or Scrum Team can write User Stories on Index Cards, including personas. When sprint planning, the Scrum Team can write specific development-related tasks on each card. The team can use actual cards or make or print a template with specific information that they want each card to include when it is taped to the board.

TIP: Your team could use different colors for each type of exercise being done. Each color could represent options such as User Stories, improvements, issues, impediments or roadblocks and tasks.

Since we are currently discussing the process of Create Tasks in the Plan and Estimate phase, Index Cards could be available in the planning room and the team could write information such as:

- *User Story #*
- *Developer Name*
- *Tester Name*
- *Revision # or some sort of numbering*
- *And the Description of the task*

PLAN and ESTIMATE	INPUTS		TOOLS		OUTPUTS	
Estimate Tasks	Scrum Core Team	*	Task Planning Meetings	*	Effort Estimated Task List	*
	Task List	*	Estimation Criteria	*	Updated Task List	
	User Story Acceptance Criteria		Planning Poker			
	Dependencies		Fist of Five			
	Identified Risks		Other Task Estimation Techniques			
	Scrum Guidance Body Recommendations					

Figure 49: A chart showing the Inputs, Tools and Outputs for the Estimate Tasks Process in the Plan and Estimate Phase.

Estimate Tasks

I believe that at this point, more and more terms of each page are becoming common place terms.

Next let's take a look at Estimate Tasks.

This is a process in the Plan and Estimate phase.

During this process, when estimating tasks, the Scrum Team must look at all the items in the task list, along with the dependencies and risks to estimate the effort required to accomplish each task in the Task List. The result of this effort is the Effort Estimated Task List.

TASKS	TASK LIST
Actionable activities	List of all committed tasks in the current sprint
Determined in the Task Planning meeting	Output for the Task Planning Meeting
Result of decomposition	

Figure 50: A chart showing Tasks vs. Task Lists.

Tasks and Task Lists

Let's look at the two key inputs starting with tasks.

ACR   Tasks are the development actions to be carried out to complete a User Story. These items may be represented with sticky notes on the board as the outcome of the Task Planning Meeting or the Sprint Planning Meeting. Tasks could be actions related to the design of a User Story, development efforts – such as performance tests, unit testing, *UAT (User Acceptance Testing)* or documentation.

The Task Planning Meeting is time-boxed to two hours per week of a sprint for ease of clarification of requirements set forth by the Customers. This meeting has two parts:

1. *Part 1, where the Product Owner suggests specific user stories for the sprint and the Scrum Team determines the total number of items that can be completed*

2. *Part 2, where the Scrum Team breaks down User Stories into tasks – otherwise known as decomposition!!*
   TIP: This too is a very important Scrum exam term!

Whereas, a Task List is the <u>OUTPUT</u> or list of ALL the individual tasks and the associated descriptions the Scrum Team has full committed to completion for a sprint.

PLAN & ESTIMATE	INPUTS		TOOLS		OUTPUTS	
Create Sprint Backlog	Scrum Core Team	*	Sprint Planning Meetings	*	Sprint Backlog	*
	Effort Estimated Task List	*	Sprint Tracking Tools		Sprint Burndown Chart	*
	Length of Sprint	*	Length of Sprint Tracking Metrics			
	Previous Sprint Velocity					
	Dependencies					
	Team Calendar					

Figure 51: *A chart showing the Inputs, Tools and Outputs for the Create Sprint Backlog Process in the Plan and Estimate Phase.*

Create Sprint Backlog

This is a process of the Plan and Estimate phase. During this process, a list of tasks are identified by the Scrum Team to be completed in the sprint. The team identifies any dependencies and tries to anticipate them accordingly. In the Sprint Planning Meeting, the team selects a number of Prioritized Product Backlog items or user stories and lists all the possible tasks by type. The Sprint Backlog may be kept electronically and include the User Story description, tasks and possibly the estimates when known.

All of these details help to determine the length of the sprints.

In order to better plan future sprints, the leadership may look at the velocity of the team as a measure, let's look at this next.

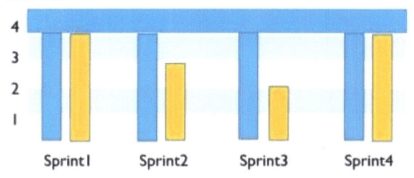

Figure 52: *A chart depicting Team Velocity.*

Team Velocity

This is an input of the Create Sprint Backlog process in the Plan and Estimate phase.

Velocity is a method for measuring the rate at which Scrum Team members consistently deliver value to the Customer. To calculate velocity of your Scrum Team, add up the estimates for the features, user stories, requirements or backlog items that were successfully delivered in each sprint versus what was committed.

The chart above depicts an example. The blue bars represent the work that was committed to by the team for that sprint; whereas the yellow or goldenrod bars show the actual amount of user stories that were completed by the team. Take a moment to look this over.

Notes:

_____

_____

_____

_____

_____

DAY 72:

Sprint Planning Meeting

This is a tool of the create Sprint Backlog process in the Plan and Estimate phase.

This meeting is facilitated by the Scrum master. During the Sprint Planning Meeting, the User Stories that are approved, estimated and committed are discussed by the Scrum Team. Each Scrum Team member uses the Effort Estimated task List to select the tasks for the current sprint.

At this time, the sprint backlog and sprint burndown chart are created - that being said, let's focus on the Sprint Burndown Chart next.

Notes:

_____

_____

_____

_____

_____

DAY 73:

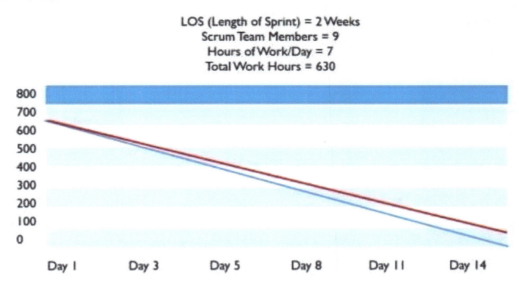

LOS (Length of Sprint) = 2 Weeks
Scrum Team Members = 9
Hours of Work/Day = 7
Total Work Hours = 630

Figure 53: *An illustration depicting the Sprint Burndown Chart.*

Sprint Burndown Chart

This is an output of the Create Sprint Backlog process in the Plan and Estimate phase.

This is a type of chart that shows the actual work remaining in the current sprint. This is used as a tracking tool. It is updated on a daily basis by the Scrum Master as the number of Total Remaining Work Hours is decreased. In the pictured illustration, the team is behind if the red line is the actual work and the blue line represents the target remaining on a given day.

This type of chart should lead the Scrum Master down the road of finding out why the team is behind. This individual should be locating the area and cause of the roadblock and help to mitigate future risks to get back on target.

This type of chart is also a close cousin to the Sprint Burnup Chart. The difference is that the Sprint Burnup Chart shows the COMPLETED work to date in a sprint.

IMPLEMENT	INPUTS		TOOLS		OUTPUTS	
Create Deliverables	Scrum Core Team	*	Team Expertise	*	Sprint Deliverables	*
	Sprint backlog	*	Software		Updated Scrumboard	*
	Scrumboard	*	Other Development Tools		Updated Impediment Log	*
	Impediment Log	*	Scrum Guidance Body Expertise		Unapproved Change Requests	
	Release Planning Schedule				Identified Risks	
	Dependencies				Mitigated Risks	
	Scrum Guidance Body Recommendations				Updated Dependencies	

Figure 54: *A chart showing the Inputs, Tools and Outputs for the Create Deliverables Process in the Implement Phase.*

KNOWLEDGE ASSESSMENT:

Epics are an Input of the _____ Process in the _____ Phase?

    A. Conduct Release Planning, Initiate
    B. **Create User Stories, Plan and Estimate**
    C. Create User Stories, Initiate
    D. None of the Above

Create Deliverables

This is a process of the Implement Phase. During this process, the Scrum Team works on tasks to create the sprint deliverables.

While development work is being done, the Scrumboard tracks progress of all the tasks committed to the sprint. While in the Daily Standup Meetings, the Scrum Master tracks any roadblocks or impediments in an Impediment Log. All activities are completed according to the total release schedule. There are two inputs we will focus on in this section: Scrumboard and Impediment Log.

The team uses their shared knowledge of development tools and knowledge of the user stories to create such deliverables. In so doing, any risks are identified and tracked.

Let's take a specific look at the Scrumboard and what that looks like.

Notes:

_____

_____

_____

_____

_____

DAY 75:

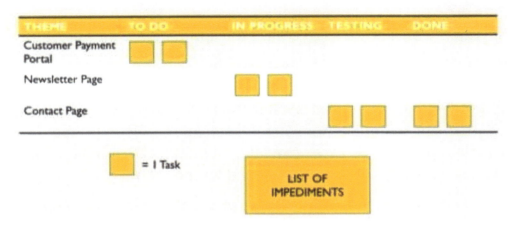

Figure 55: *An image similar to the Scrumboard.*

Scrumboard

This is an input of the Create Deliverables process in the Implement phase. It is an artifact of the Daily Standup Meeting that tracks progress in a sprint. The Scrumboard is a physical board in a dedicated conference room that contains four working columns:

1. *To Do – for items that have not been started*

2. *In Progress – for items or tasks that have been started but have not yet been through any kind of testing*

3. *Testing – for tasks that are being tested at the moment*

4. *Done – for tasks that are in a completed task and are waiting to be demoed at the next Sprint Review Meeting*

The items are actually tasks or actionable items in the user stories that could be in the form of sticky notes stuck onto a whiteboard. All tasks are grouped across rows by theme.

The Scrumboard is wiped clean at the end of each sprint in preparation for the next sprint's details during the Daily Standup Meetings.

Figure 56: *Impediments STOP positive project progress.*

Impediment Log

This is also an input of the Create Deliverables process in the Implement phase. Much like a **stop sign** stops the flow of traffic, this is a log or listing of roadblocks that stop, slow or impede development efforts with regard to task completion. The log is typically tracked either on the side of the Scrumboard or in another visible location electronically for anyone to access. The team must realize that impediments are inevitable and should be mitigated. There is no such thing as a project without impediments, it is all in how they are handled and solved.

Typically the log includes information or columns such as the following:

- *Title/Theme*
- *Priority of Fix*
- *Assigned To*
- *Status*
- *Notes*

The next thing you might ask is, *"What is an example of an impediment to a project?"* Well, I am glad you asked! An impediment could be a lack of technical knowledge, question about a requirement, external factor such as organizational changes, management challenges, modifications to process and more.

IMPLEMENT	INPUTS		TOOLS		OUTPUTS	
Conduct Daily Standup	Scrum Core Team	*	Daily Standup Meeting	*	Updated Sprint Burndown Chart	*
	Scrum Master	*	Three Daily Questions	*	Updated Impediment Log	*
	Sprint Burndown Chart	*	War Room		Motivated Scrum Team	
	Impediment Log	*	Video Conferencing		Updated Scrumboard	
	Product Owner				Unapproved Change Requests	
	Previous Work Day Experience				Identified Risks	
	Scrumboard				Mitigated Risks	
	Dependencies				Updated Dependencies	

Figure 57: *A chart showing the Inputs, Tools and Outputs for the Conduct Daily Standup Process in the Implement Phase.*

Conduct Daily Standup

This is a process of the Implement phase. The Daily Standup Meeting is held at the same time in the same place. There is one term that may or may not be new to you and that is War Room. That said, let's look into this tool.

DAY 78:

TOOLS	
Daily Standup Meeting	*
Three Daily Questions	*
War Room	
Video Conferencing	

Figure 58: War Room is a Tool for the Conduct Daily Standup Process in the Implement Phase.

War Room

A War Room is the term used for the place where the developers or Scrum Team members convene to work. This may be a dedicated room or a cube area. Nonetheless, it is an area where the team can work closely under good lighting. It is deemed as a place that is conducive to sharing ideas and helping less experienced members so they can get up to speed.

You are in the home stretch!

KNOWLEDGE ASSESSMENT:

Which of the following is <u>NOT</u> a column of the Scrumboard?

   A. Done
   B. In Progress
   C. Testing
   D. Accepted

IMPLEMENT	INPUTS	TOOLS	OUTPUTS
Groom Prioritized Product Backlog	Scrum Core Team *	Prioritized Product * Backlog Review Meetings	Updated * Prioritized Product Backlog
	Prioritized Product * Backlog	Communications Techniques	Updated Release Planning Schedule
	Rejected Deliverables	Other Prioritized Product Backlog Techniques	
	Approved Change Requests		
	Unapproved Change Requests		
	Identified Risks		
	Updated Program Product Backlog		
	Retrospect Sprint Logs		
	Dependencies		
	Release Planning Schedule		
	Scrum Guidance Body Recommendations		

Figure 59: *A chart showing the Inputs, Tools and Outputs for the Groom Prioritized Product Backlog Process in the Implement Phase.*

Groom Prioritized Product Backlog

This is a final process of the Implement phase.

Before we get started, you notice that even more of the terms of this page have since become familiar and maybe even common place for you!

In this process the Prioritized Product Backlog is constantly updated in each sprint. The word groom means to refine or update. At this point, a meeting called the Prioritized Product Backlog Review Meeting is held. The intent of such a meeting is to update the backlog based on recent changes or additions. This could include User Stories that were rejected by the Product Owner in a previous sprint or items that were added by a Stakeholder in a Sprint Review (demo) Meeting.

I think by now you can see a pattern that oftentimes the output of one process ends up being the input for a following process. You are doing great!! Keep up the positive progress towards learning and absorbing all that you can about Scrum and the phases and processes!

Notes:

_____

_____

_____

_____

_____

DAY 80:

REVIEW and RETROSPECT	INPUTS	TOOLS	OUTPUTS
Convene Scrum of Scrums	Scrum Master or Scrum Team Representatives *	Scrum of Scrum Meeting *	Better Team Coordination *
	Chief Scrum Master	Four Questions per Team *	Resolved Issues
	Chief Product Owner	Video Conferencing	Updated Impediment Log
	Meeting Agenda	Meeting Room	Updated Dependencies
	Impediment Log	Scrum Guidance Body Expertise	
	Dependencies		
	Outputs from Retrospect Sprint		

Figure 60: A chart showing the Inputs, Tools and Outputs for the Convene Scrum of Scrums Process in the Review and Retrospect Phase.

Notes:

_____

_____

_____

_____

_____

Convene Scrum of Scrums

This is a process of the Review and Retrospect phase.

We talked on a previous page about what the Scrum of Scrums is, but it has been a while, so let's review. The Scrum of Scrums is only used in projects that are larger in scale. The Scrum Guidance Body outlines what 'large in scale' truly means to the company or organization.

The Scrum of Scrums is a meeting that may or may not have a regular frequency. It is facilitated by the Chief Scrum Master. There are four questions asked in his meeting of all attendees. It is much like the Daily Standup Meeting, except that the intent is to gain a wide view of the progress of multiple teams and the dependencies. This type of meeting is not set to be daily as it takes a lot of coordination.

The next page will mention more, as well as those four magic questions.

Notes:

_____

_____

_____

_____

_____

The Scrum of Scrums is a meeting in a regular meeting room where the Scrum Master or a representative from the Scrum Team of multiple teams convene to share progress on items that may have an effect on one or more teams in a larger project. This meeting is <u>NOT</u> a time-boxed meeting. The word time-boxed, as you may already know, refer to whether the meeting or activity has a maximum time frame to which to be complete.

ACR   The *Scrum of Scrums or SOS*, is much like the Daily Standup Meeting of a single Scrum Team. However, the single Scrum Team daily standup has three questions; whereas, the Scrum of Scrums has four questions asked of each representative:

1.) *What has my team been working on since the last meeting?*
2.) *What will my team do until the next meeting?*
3.) *What, if any, items that other teams may be counting on our team to finish that remains undone?*
4.) *What is our team planning to do that might affect other teams?*

The purpose of this meeting is to foster more efficient communication amongst teams, talk about dependencies and identify large-scaled risks in a timely manner.

This meeting is held at a pre-determined frequency and may be conducted via video conference, especially if one or more representatives work from a remote location.

You have made it a long way!

REVIEW and RETROSPECT	INPUTS		TOOLS		OUTPUTS	
Demonstrate and Validate Sprint	Scrum Core Team	*	Sprint Review Meetings	*	Accepted Deliverables	*
	Sprint Deliverables	*	EVA		Rejected Deliverables	
	Sprint Backlog	*	Scrum Guidance Body Expertise		Updated Risks	
	Done Criteria	*			EVA Results (actual vs. Planned performance)	
	User Story Acceptance Criteria	*			Updated Release Planning Schedule	
	Stakeholders				Updated Dependencies	
	Release Planning Schedule					
	Identified Risks					
	Dependencies					
	Scrum Guidance Body Recommendations					

Figure 61: *A chart showing the Inputs, Tools and Outputs for the Demonstrate and Validate Sprint Process in the Review and Retrospect Phase.*

Demonstrate and Validate Sprint

This is a process of the Review and Retrospect Sprint phase.

This process includes three practices:

1. *Sprint Review Meeting*

2. *Accepted Deliverables*

3. *Rejected or Unapproved Deliverables*

We will look at the Sprint Review Meeting on the next page, but this is where the Product Owner inspects the User Stories completed in the sprint and either accepts or rejects them based on the Acceptance Criteria set forth. This meeting is held at the end of each sprint. It is a time where developers and testers show the potentially shippable increment or product created in the sprint. The Stakeholders and Customers have a chance to provide feedback.

As for the second item in the list of Accepted Deliverables, if the Product Owner approves, the increment can be released to the Customer. At that point, a list of accepted features are created and kept when delivered to the Customer.

Finally, the rejected items. These are the items that are added back to the prioritized product backlog for a future sprint. Notice that I did NOT say that they are added to the NEXT sprint, but instead I mentioned a FUTURE sprint.

Notes:

_____

_____

_____

_____

_____

DAY 83:

TOOLS

Sprint Review Meetings *

Earned Value Analysis

Scrum Guidance Body Expertise

Figure 62: *Sprint Review Meetings is a Tool for the Demonstrate and Validate Sprint Process in the Review and Retrospect Phase.*

Sprint Review Meetings

This is a tool of the Demonstrate and Validate Sprint process in the Review and Retrospect phase.

The Sprint Review Meeting happens at the end of each sprint. It provides a means for the Scrum Team to demo the work completed in the sprint. There are several things that happen in this meeting:

1. *A member of the team or the Scrum Master provides a demo of the functionality to the Product Owner, Stakeholders and Customers*
2. *The Product Owner approves or rejects the User Stories based on the Acceptance Criteria. If approved, the story is complete. If rejected, the story is added back to the Prioritized Product Backlog for incorporation in a future sprint.*

This meeting is time-boxed to four hours per one-month sprint.

Now let's take a closer look at the breakdown of the Retrospect Sprint process.

Nicely done!

DAY 84:

REVIEW & RETROSPECT	INPUTS	TOOLS	OUTPUTS
Retrospect Sprint	Scrum Master *	Retrospect Sprint Meeting *	Agreed Actionable Improvements *
	Scrum Team	ESVP	Assigned Action Items and Due Dates
	Outputs from Demonstrate and Validate Sprint	Speed Boat	Proposed Non-Functional Items for Prioritized Product Backlog
	Product Owner	Metrics and Measuring Techniques	Retrospect Sprint Logs
	Scrum Guidance Body Recommendations	Scrum Guidance Body Expertise	Scrum Team Lessons Learned
			Updated Scrum Guidance Body Recommendations

Figure 63: *A chart showing the Inputs, Tools and Outputs for the Retrospect Sprint Process in the Review and Retrospect Phase.*

Retrospect Sprint

This is a process in the Review and Retrospect phase.

During this process, there are several tools that can be used in the retrospect meeting to take a look at the lessons learned. This meeting is typically attended by the Scrum Team and Scrum Master. Notice that the Stakeholders and Customers are <u>NOT</u> in attendance.

The goal of this meeting high-level is to come away with lessons learned, as in what could be improved upon in the following sprint. These items are tracked in a log and referenced throughout the remainder of the project. It is a good idea to be specific in this log complete with actionable items and associated date.

The next few pages will be dedicated to tools that can be used to gauge user interest, keep attendees engaged and to identify steps or process that recently held the team back.

The first is ESVP.

Continue to study and learn lots!

Notes:

_____

_____

_____

_____

_____

EXPLORER	SHOPPER
VACATIONER	PRISONER

Figure 64: *A table showing what ESVP stands for in terms of the acronym.*

ESVP

This is a tool used in the Retrospect Sprint process of the Review and Retrospect phase.

This is an acronym and an anonymous strategy to be used at the start of the Retrospect Sprint Meeting to poll the audience so to speak to gauge the mind of the attendees.

ACR The Scrum Master may hand out sticky notes or some other means for gathering responses – and they must be anonymous. The options for response include the following:

1. *An EXPLORER wants to seek answers and always learn from the meeting*

2. *A SHOPPER listens and chooses the information to take away from the meeting or process*

3. *A VACATIONER wants to relax and be a tourist during the discussions*

4. *A PRISONER is only in the meeting because they are being forced by requirement*

Next, let's look at the term Speedboat.

DAY 86:

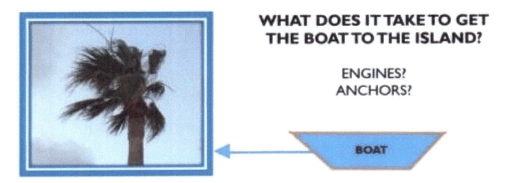

Figure 65: *An illustration of Speedboat.*

Speedboat

This is another tool used in the Retrospect Sprint process of the Review and Retrospect phase.

Speedboat is a term and technique used in the Retrospect Sprint Meeting. This activity is actually time-boxed to just a few minutes to identify accomplishments and roadblocks. Here is how it works:

All of the attendees pretend to be the crew of the boat. The tree stands for an island, which is an illustration of metaphor for the Project Vision Statement. The boat is the tool to get the team to reach the island. The team is to quickly and anonymously write on sticky notes the engines and anchors. If you can picture this scenario, an engine helps you to make progress or progress towards a goal or destination.

In our illustration, the engines to be written would include any activity that supported the vision statement of the project. The anchors (perhaps to be written on a different colored sticky note) are to be any impediments (solved or not) that have stood in the way for the team or one of the members.

This activity quickly and efficiently illustrates, once tallied, the big picture of the recent sprint now that it has come to a close. Keep in mind that in a retrospect meeting, the goal is to determine what work and what we should discontinue doing. It also tells us what needs improving as well. The outcome of such a meeting would be to come up with actionable items for the next sprint or project.

With that being said, let's take a look at the Retrospect Sprint Meeting.

EXCELLENT work!

_____
_____
_____
_____
_____

KNOWLEDGE ASSESSMENT:

True or False: Rejected items from the Sprint Review Meeting are automatically added to the NEXT sprint?

   A. True
   B. False

DAY 87:

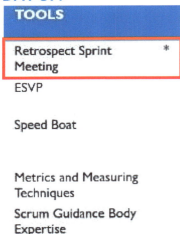

Figure 66: *Retrospect Sprint Meeting is a Tool for the Retrospect Sprint Process in the Review and Retrospect Phase.*

Retrospect Sprint Meeting

This is the final tool we will discuss in the Retrospect Sprint process of the Review and Retrospect Sprint phase.

Not to confuse you, but there is a Retrospect Sprint Meeting AND a Retrospect Project Meeting. This page is about the sprint.

This meeting is time-boxed to four hours for a one-month sprint. It provides a means for looking back at the activities of the past or most recent sprint and analyzing what worked and what needs to be improved upon for the next sprint. It is also seen as an opportunity for success reflection and lessons learned. The output is a list of actionable items. Stakeholders and Customers are not involved in this meeting.

RELEASE	INPUTS		TOOLS		OUTPUTS	
Ship Deliverables	Product Owner	*	Organizational Deployment Methods	*	Working Deliverables Agreement	*
	Stakeholders	*	Communication Plan		Working Deliverables	
	Accepted Deliverables	*			Product Releases	
	Release Planning Schedule	*				
	Scrum Master					
	Scrum Team					
	User Story Acceptance Criteria					
	Piloting Plan					
	Scrum Guidance Body Recommendations					

Figure 67: *A chart showing the Inputs, Tools and Outputs for the Ship Deliverables Process in the Release Phase.*

Knowledge matters – keep going!

Ship Deliverables

This is a process of the Release phase.

The Release phase focuses on deploying and delivering Accepted Deliverables to the Customer or end user base. This is done by documenting the lessons learned throughout the lifecycle of the project.

In the Ship Deliverables process, the Working Deliverables Agreement provides testament as to the completion of all sprint events and activities.

You are already making a difference!

Notes:

_____

_____

_____

_____

_____

OUTPUTS
Working Deliverables   * Agreement
Working Deliverables
Product Releases

Figure 68: Working Deliverables is an Output for the Ship Deliverables Process in the Release Phase.

Working Deliverables

This is an output of the Ship Deliverables process of the Release phase.

These are the final, deployed products to the end users. In a more detailed look, the Scrum Team works a task affiliated with a user story in the sprint backlog to ultimately create a working deliverable. The tasks each outline the work to be done until the functionality meets the requirements known to the Product Owner.

Upon approval, the mode of delivery is selected and the project or product is implemented. These deliverables receive final sign-off as well as approval in the Working Deliverables Agreement on behalf of the Customer and/or the Executive Project Sponsor.

Notes:

_____

_____

_____

_____

_____

DAY 90:

RELEASE	INPUTS	TOOLS	OUTPUTS
Retrospect Project	Scrum Core Team *	Retrospect Project Meeting *	Agreed Actionable Improvements *
	Chief Scrum Master	Other Tools for Retrospect Project	Assigned Action Items and Due Dates *
	Chief Product owner	Scrum Guidance Body Expertise	Proposed Non-Functional Items for Program Product Backlog and Prioritized Product Backlog
	Stakeholders		Updated Scrum Guidance Body Recommendations
	Scrum Guidance Body Recommendations		

Figure 69: A chart showing the Inputs, Tools and Outputs for the Retrospect Project Process in the Release Phase.

Retrospect Project

This is a process in the Release phase.

Retrospect Project is a process of the Release phase and includes a meeting held at the end of the project on behalf of the Scrum Team Members and, optionally, the Stakeholders. This Scrum Team works as a team to not only convene at a specific time and location, but also to document and track the lessons learned or 'takeaways.'

When we look at the Tools for this process, we note that the Scrum Guidance Body can be consulted for specific processes as questions arise.

The outputs of the Retrospect Project process is documentation of the Agreed Actionable Improvements for future projects, action items and assignments.

If there are any functional items that are discovered and not addressed in a current User Story, then these items can be added to the Prioritized Product Backlog for incorporation in future sprints as well.

Notes:

_____

_____

_____

_____

_____

DAY 91:

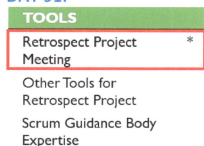

TOOLS
Retrospect Project Meeting *
Other Tools for Retrospect Project
Scrum Guidance Body Expertise

Figure 70: Retrospect Project Meeting is a Tool for the Retrospect Project Process in the Release Phase.

Retrospect Project Meeting

This is a tool of the Retrospect Project process of the Release phase.

We already looked at the Retrospect Sprint Meeting AND the Retrospect Project process, now let's look at the project in retrospect.

This meeting is <u>NOT</u> time-boxed, unlike the Retrospect Sprint Meeting. It provides a means for looking back at the activities of the past or most recent project and analyzing what and what was not successful, what to change the next time around and the items that are not in the current scope. It is also seen as an opportunity for success reflection and lessons learned. The Output is actionable items. Stakeholders and Customers are not involved in this meeting.

Notes:

_____

_____

_____

_____

_____

Scrum is a type of Agile methodology – the most popular methodologies of those listed on-screen. There are however, other Agile approaches, which include the following:

1. *Kanban/Lean*
2. *XP*
3. *DSDM*
4. *Crystal and*
5. *FDD*

To be agile is the ability to change direction at a rapid pace in a consistent manner.

So, now let's see an overview of each of these approaches (otherwise known as methodologies) of Agile.

Getting closer to the end of this book!

Notes:

_____

_____

_____

_____

_____

Kanban/Lean	XP	DSDM	Crystal	FDD
Limits items that are in the WIP or Work in Progress status "Signboard" Taiichi Ohno Use of visual tools, such as task cards, Scrumboards and Burndown Charts	1990s Originated in Chrysler Corporation Managing costs Values simplicity and feedback Engineering practices	1995 framework; later version in 2007 called DSDM Atern Administered by the DSDM Consortium MoSCoW System-oriented Six Phases	1990s Alistair Cockburn People-centric Use of color spectrum	Also known as Test-First Development Kent Beck, a creator of XP Two Levels: ATDD (Acceptance TDD) and DTDD (Developer TDD)

Figure 71: *A chart comparing several Agile Methodologies.*

Agile Methodologies

This will be a little longer topic!

Today we will detail several other Agile methodologies.

Kanban or Lean:

This methodology limits that amount of tasks or items that are in progress and reduces waste. The tool used is much like the Scrumboard, but referred to as a signboard. Several of the same artifacts are used as in Scrum.

XP:

ACR *XP stands for Extreme programming.* This methodology was first developed in the 1990s originating with the Chrysler Corporation regarding engineering practices. The goal was to manage costs of a project. The core value of this methodology centers around simplicity or simplifying work and gaining consistent feedback. The roles in this methodology are, the Customer, developer, tracker and coach.

DSDM:

ACR *DSDM stands for Dynamic Systems Development Method.* This method was developed in 1995 with a later version in 2007 called DSDM Atern. It was initially administered by the DSDM Consortium. The idea behind this methodology is that it encourages continual improvement while focusing on cost, quality and time. It uses a prioritization method that you are familiar with called MoSCoW.

Crystal:

An agile methodology first introduced in the 1990s by Alistair Cockburn as a people-centric methodology. The color spectrum is used based on the scope and size of the project. The colors range from Crystal Clear for smaller projects working through larger projects, which are classified by Crystal Diamond or Crystal Sapphire.

FDD:

ACR *FDD stands for Feature-Driven Development.* For this methodology, know that Kent Beck, creator of XP first introduced this methodology, which is also referred to as Test-First Development.

As shown in the previous table, there are two levels: ATDD and DTDD.

The next thing we want to discuss is what the roles are within the Scrum framework.

DAY 94:

SCRUM	WATERFALL/ TRADITIONAL PROJECT MANAGEMENT
People-Oriented	Process-Oriented
Minimal documentation	Complex Documentation
Sprint vs. Upfront Planning	Upfront Planning
Project Requirements Based on Business Value	Based on Project Plan
	Managed Team Organization
Self-Organizing Team	Centralized Management
Decentralized Management	

Figure 72: A chart comparing Scrum vs. Waterfall or Traditional Project Management.

Scrum vs. Waterfall

Now that you know what Scrum is and how it is used at a high level, let's talk about how Scrum compares to the traditional project management method or Waterfall.

Scrum Approach

Starting with Scrum, this is a people-oriented methodology. It promotes the ability to adapt quickly to change by planning at the beginning of each sprint, not the beginning of the project. This methodology will always leave room for documentation, but it is just not the focus. The focus of Scrum projects is the concentrate on continually offering value to the Customer based on what the Customer deems as important. A Scrum Team is a self-organizing team, by where everyone teaches the other members and the Scrum Master is more of a facilitator than a Project Manager. Finally, the management style of the leadership is decentralized, versus the focus being on a singular, dominating leader.

Waterfall Approach

Let's contrast this with the Waterfall approach.

This methodology is focused on the process as a whole that is heavy in documentation, but also upfront planning. The governing document is the project plan, which is often created in a project planning software or spreadsheet for tracking. A Waterfall project has a Project Manager that manages the expectations, relationships and ultimately the work. The Stakeholder is less involved in this approach until the end of the project. The management is centralized putting a lot of project ownership on the Project Manager.

Both the Scrum Master and Project Manager are management roles!

This brings us to the end of the content. Over the next few days, we will summarize what you learned and have a few practice tests to test your knowledge.

Notes:

_____

_____

_____

_____

_____

KNOWLEDGE ASSESSMENT:

True or False: The Retrospect Project Meeting is time-boxed?

    A. True
    B. **False**

DAY 95:

CONGRATULATIONS!

Congratulations on completing this course! It is up to you the course of action from here. I believe that if you pick up the SBOK guide at this point, the majority of the details in the several hundred pages now seem much more familiar!

In summary, this course covered the following:

1. *Discussed an overview of Scrum practices – including what is Scrum and what are the members of the Scrum core team*

2. *Learned Scrum principles – these consist of Empirical Process Control, Self-Organization, Collaboration, Value-Based Prioritization, Time-Boxing and Iterative Development*

3. *Discussed Scrum aspects – which include Organization, Business Justification, Quality, Change and Risk*

4. *Defined Scrum phases – including Initiate, Plan and Estimate, Implement, Review and Retrospect and Release*

5. *Informed you of the 19 Scrum processes*

6. *Gained a basic understanding of several other Agile methodologies*

Practice Exam 1

1. Task List is a Process for which Phase?
   a. **Plan and Estimate**
   b. Release
   c. Implement
   d. Initiate

2. Retrospect Sprint is a Process for which Phase?
   a. Plan and Estimate
   b. Release
   c. **Review and Retrospect**
   d. Initiate

3. Identify Tasks is a Process for which Phase?
   a. **Plan and Estimate**
   b. Release
   c. Implement
   d. Initiate

4. Ship Deliverables is a Process for which Phase?
   a. Plan and Estimate
   b. **Release**
   c. Implement
   d. Initiate

5. Retrospect Project is a Process for which Phase?
   a. Plan and Estimate
   b. **Release**
   c. Implement
   d. Initiate

DAY 97:
Practice Exam 2

1. Which of the following is <u>NOT</u> a Scrum Principle?
   - a. Self-Organization
   - b. Collaboration
   - **c. Change**
   - d. Empirical Process Control

2. Which of the following is <u>NOT</u> a Scrum Principle?
   - a. Value-Based Prioritization
   - b. Iterative Development
   - c. Collaboration
   - **d. Risk**

3. Transparency, Inspection and Adaptation are all keywords to which of the following Scrum Principles?
   - a. Self-Organization
   - b. Collaboration
   - c. Iterative Development
   - **d. Empirical Process Control**

4. Which of the following <u>IS</u> a Scrum Aspect?
   - **a. Business Justification**
   - b. Project Vision Statement
   - c. Self-Organization
   - d. Time-Boxing

Practice Exam 3

1. Lessons Learned are a result of which type of meeting?
    a. **Retrospect**
    b. Release
    c. Task Planning
    d. Sprint Planning

2. How many columns are to be on a Scrumboard?
    a. 3
    b. **4**
    c. 5
    d. None of the Above

3. Which of the following is a Process-Oriented methodology?
    a. **Waterfall**
    b. Scrum
    c. Both of the Above
    d. None of the Above

4. Awareness, Articulation and Appropriation are key terms belonging to which of the following Scrum Principles?
    a. Self-Organization
    b. **Collaboration**
    c. Change
    d. Empirical Process Control

Quick Reference 1

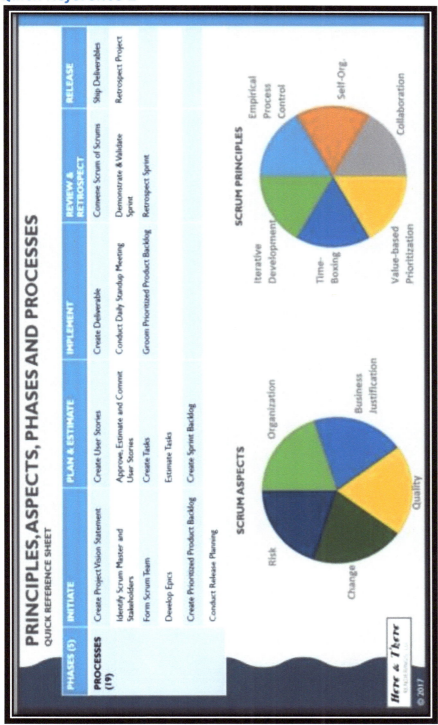

USER STORIES
QUICK REFERENCE SHEET

INDEPENDENT

NEGOTIABLE
Should be able to stand-alone so that it can be split or reprioritized

VALUABLE
Know why it IS or IS NOT valuable to the customer

ESTIMATABLE
Determine if a value can be assessed to aid in prioritization

SMALL
Keep the wording short, yet detailed enough to formulate the tasks and Acceptance Criteria

TESTABLE
There is enough information to test in isolation and as part of the whole if developed and tested by someone else

WHY?
User Stories avoid confusion regarding requirements and help put a face to a feature through the use of personas.

GOAL:
A well-written User Story contains Acceptance Criteria to help the Product Owner determine completion in the Sprint Review Meeting.

EXAMPLE:
The employee portal that includes training classes currently suppresses past courses taken. User would like to be able to review course content as a refresher – instead of only seeing that they completed the curriculum.

USER STORY
As an employee, I want to be able to review the content of past courses in my training plan to reduce time in outside research.

ACCEPTANCE CRITERIA
1. Historical Page Creation
2. Completed courses are NOT suppressed

Here & There

© 2017

126